PRAISE FOR *THE TWENTYSOMETHING GUIDE TO GETTING IT TOGETHER*

"If I'd had this brilliant book to gently guide me through my twenties, I absolutely would have gotten a lot more done, a lot less drunk. I desperately hope Mary Traina writes one of these for every decade."

—Jessi Klein
Writer/Comedian
Inside Amy Schumer (Head Writer)

"If you're a twentysomething who's stuck in a rut you need this book. And if you are a twentysomething let's face it: You're probably in a rut. Mary Traina is like a contract killer. Her targets? Your dead-end job, your toxic love life, and your own worst enemy: yourself."

—George Northy
Writer
G.B.F., MTV's *Faking It*

"This guide is a must-read for everyone in their twenties. Even if you know what a 401(k) is and you finally stopped hooking up with that dude with the man bun, Mary Traina will make you laugh and inspire you to level up in all areas of your life. This book is essentially an anthology of all the real-life pep talks Mary gave me throughout my twenties and I emerged, if not like a butterfly from a cocoon, relatively unscathed and without crippling Madewell debt (thanks for talking me out of those pants, Mary)."

—Alison Bennett
Television Writer
FX's *You're The Worst*, Amazon's *Betas*, MTV's *Hey Girl*

"There are lots of things nobody tells you about your mid-to-late twenties—not even your best friend, your attentive therapist, your understanding boyfriend, your nagging mother, or your cool cousin. This book fills the role of all those people (and more!). Take it from someone who lived through all these adventures with the author herself."

—Andrew Hampp
Senior Correspondent
Billboard Magazine

"Mary's advice feels like you've got your own fairy godmother watching out for you through the highs and lows of new adulthood. It is exactly what every twentysomething needs to hear in a friendly, approachable, and laugh-out-loud manner."

—Kourtney Jason
Coauthor of *Lights Camera Booze* and Managing Editor of Life2PointOh.com

A STEP-BY-STEP PLAN FOR SURVIVING YOUR
QUARTERLIFE CRISIS

THE 20 SOMETHING guide to GETTING IT TOGETHER

Mary Traina
Blogger for HelloGiggles

△adamsmedia
Avon, Massachusetts

305. 242
TRA

54715107

Published by
Adams Media, a division of F+W Media, Inc.
57 Littlefield Street, Avon, MA 02322. U.S.A.
www.adamsmedia.com

ISBN 10: 1-4405-7183-X
ISBN 13: 978-1-4405-7183-1
eISBN 10: 1-4405-7184-8
eISBN 13: 978-1-4405-7184-8

Printed in the United States of America.

10 9 8 7 6 5 4 3 2 1

Library of Congress Cataloging-in-Publication Data

Traina, Mary.
The twentysomething guide to getting it together / Mary Traina.
    pages cm
Includes index.
ISBN 978-1-4405-7183-1 (pb) -- ISBN 1-4405-7183-X (pb) -- ISBN 978-1-4405-7184-8
(ebook) -- ISBN 1-4405-7184-8 (ebook)
1. Young adults--Life skills guides. 2. Young adults--Conduct of life. I. Title.
HQ799.5.T717 2014
646.70084'2--dc23
                                    2014009081

Cover design by Stephanie Hannus.
Cover images © Sergii Kostenko/123RF; antishock/123RF.

This book is available at quantity discounts for bulk purchases.
For information, please call 1-800-289-0963.

DEDICATION

To all the strong, inspiring
women in my family.

ACKNOWLEDGMENTS

At my most turbulent moments, reading has brought me comfort and made me feel less alone. Novelists, bloggers, journalists, Internet commentators, friends who e-mail—they've all inspired me to reach out and connect through writing.

I'm grateful to everyone at HelloGiggles for giving me the opportunity to write my *Late 20s Rut-Busting* series and my great friend Alison Bennett for getting me in the door and teaching me what it means to be bold. I am forever in debt to my literary agent, Allison Cohen, who saw potential in me and continues to champion me. Huge thanks to my editor Katie Corcoran Lytle, Maria Ribas, and everyone at Adams Media who helped shape my twentysomething foibles into something I'm proud of.

This book would be half as long without my rock, Lindsy Serrano, who learned all these lessons along with me, and Deanna Michalopoulos, who always knew just what to say when I hit a wall. This book would be missing a certain amount of zen had I never met Jason Selvig, who taught me how to enjoy life in each moment. And this book would have lacked a happy ending if it weren't for my amazing friends, who contributed stories and cheered me on. I'm thankful to have met people with whom I can laugh through our problems. Special thanks to Andrew Hampp, Joseph Gerard, Ben Cochran, and "Striketopus," my championship bowling team, for your support.

I'd also like to thank my loving, funny, and supportive immediate family: Kathy, John, Danielle, and Andrea. Your natural ability to just be who you are has given me the strength to do the same.

CONTENTS

INTRODUCTION

Do you feel like you spend *all* your time at work but aren't any closer to realizing your career goals than you were when you first applied? Do you feel like every time you are about to go to the gym, Netflix beckons you to binge-watch? Were you kinda assuming financial stability would miraculously happen by the time you were thirty, but now it seems more likely you'll have to claw your way out of debt using only self-control? If any of this sounds like you, then you are not alone—you are a twentysomething. And like most twentysomethings, you've hit a point where you've grown tired of the struggle and are ready to take responsibility for your life and move forward to the world of savings accounts, restful nights, and clean laundry. But where do you begin?

Perhaps you've fantasized about faking your own death and starting over with a clean slate on a tropical island. But the reality is that beautiful, tropical islands are full of big, terrifying bugs . . . and the only way out of your problems is through them. You need to actively work at achieving the balance you desire. Fortunately, *The Twentysomething Guide to Getting It Together* offers all the info you need to take control of your life. In Part 1, we'll break down common ruts and examine the reasons twentysomethings slip into them. You'll get tips on how to find motivation and make room in your life for real change. In Part 2, we'll examine ways to get it together in specific areas: middling careers, neglected health, toxic friendships, lame romances, and lingering debt. Along the way, you'll read about the real life struggles of other twentysomethings, learn some fun "facts," and get pro tips for when you want to take your rut-busting up a notch.

When people say your twenties are difficult, they mean your whole twenties. They don't mean that by your mid-twenties you miraculously find all the answers. No, you have to hunt those answers down if you want to become a fully independent, successful, and fulfilled adult. This book will help you fight your fears and take control. Let's get started.

PART 1

GETTING READY TO GET IT TOGETHER

You have to make room in your life for change; otherwise it's easy to just keep falling back into bad habits. You need inspiration. That's why this section will focus on time management and actionable tips for positive thinking—to make sure these changes stick. It will also examine the mentalities that got you into those all-too-common twentysomething ruts and how to avoid repeating the same, poor decisions moving forward. So let's go! The best way to kick off the next phase of your life is with a healthy dose of self-reflection.

CHAPTER 1

Examining Your Rut: What Happened? And What Now?

You've always had the best intentions, and maybe you really want to change your life. But what is it they say about good intentions? Oh, I know . . . the road to hell is paved with them. For a lot of twentysomethings, it's hard to sacrifice the instant gratification at their fingertips in the name of success and fulfillment that is still around the corner. For example, maybe it's difficult for you to fall in love without blowing off your friends. Or maybe you tend to put a lot of thought into starting a workout routine first thing Monday morning . . . but never seem to find the time to get to the gym.

As uncomfortable as it is to look at your mistakes, the only way to get it together is by understanding where and why you went wrong. Otherwise, history has a way of repeating itself. In this chapter, you'll take a look at the factors that led you off track and learn how you can find the motivation to prioritize change, starting today. In the spirit of good intentions, allow me to first recommend an attitude adjustment: the tried-and-true Twentysomething Attitude Adjustment.

THE TWENTYSOMETHING ATTITUDE ADJUSTMENT

There comes a point in your twenties when you must shed your ego and leave your preconceived attitudes about being a responsible adult at the door. It's either that or suffer a slow descent into your parents' basement for the rest of your days. An attitude adjustment is necessary because, after a lifetime spent in the comforting embrace of family and the friends who had to hang out with you because they were stuck in your chemistry class, your thought process is most likely not wired for adulthood. You're wired to pass the next test, not build a career. You want everyone to think you're fun, not reliable. But it's time to grow up and move on, so let's examine the adolescent attitudes that often linger and become major hindrances to success in your twenties.

OUTDATED ATTITUDE: You Are Focused on Short-Term Satisfaction

Growing up, you measure your life in increments of a few years at a time: elementary school, middle school, high school, college . . . there is a built-in reset button, and it can be difficult to rewire your mind to think about your long-term goals and desired successes. Have you seen that episode of *Seinfeld* where a fire alarm goes off while George is at a child's birthday party? In order to get out the door as quickly as possible, he pushes the children and elderly people out of his path. In your early twenties, you are George, and things like bills and going to the gym are the children and elderly people. Like George, you are panicky, selfish, and have trouble slowing down to do things correctly. If you can convince yourself that happy hour is actually a valuable "networking opportunity," you're more than willing to push a tedious task like hitting the gym right out of the way.

This shortsighted decision making has a ripple effect. Instead of building a foundation of good habits, you're left without any structure at all. Instead of building up your credit and ensuring that you'll one day have financial flexibility, you've plunged yourself into devastating credit card debt to avoid minor financial sacrifices. Next time the fire alarm goes off, take a deep breath and think long term.

ATTITUDE ADJUSTMENT: Focus on Your Foundation for Long-Term Success

Responsibilities aren't obstacles you can run around or handle later; they are the key to reaching your long-term goals. So swallow your fears, and immediately handle the obstacles that stand between you and long-term success. After all, if you cut too many corners, you'll end up going in circles. When the figurative fire alarm goes off, stop and think before you run for your life: What course of action *won't* bite you in the ass later? Let's say you need to call your landlord to discuss a rent increase. It may seem easier to just ignore that headache, pay the extra rent you can't afford, and then handle your debt when you are inevitably a millionaire. Problem solved, as soon as Mark Zuckerberg sees your potential! Except, let's be real. Nobody is coming to save you. Millionaires don't get rich by bailing out twentysomethings. You're going to have to fight your battles one at a time. What you need to do is call up your landlord to negotiate your rent before it's too late.

Building up the strength to make tough choices with long-term success in mind is a valuable foundation to have. Think of it this way: Free throws become second nature to basketball players only after they've put in hundreds of hours of practice. Similarly, if you don't practice handling your problems head-on, you'll never make your free throws. Don't lie to yourself in order to make choices that suit you in the short term. Own your decisions, understand the real reasons you are making them, and hold yourself accountable when, say, you wake up hung-over instead of ready to take on the day. Good habits can be just as addictive as bad ones—and much more fulfilling. The only way to get control of your life is to buck up, buckle down, and handle yo' shit. No more excuses.

TWENTYSOMETHING FACT(ish)

If a shark stops moving, it dies. Similarly, if a twentysomething logs in to Netflix for just one episode, he will never make it to the gym.

OUTDATED ATTITUDE: F.O.M.O.

Oh, the dreaded F.O.M.O, also known as "The Fear Of Missing Out." As you begin to shoulder all the responsibilities that come along with being an independent adult, you take a look at all the amazing things your friends are doing, and you rebel against those responsibilities. You have to scrub your toilet bowl how often now? Gross! You have to buy stamps? Get real! You see your old friends from school posting about lives that seem fabulous, at least on Facebook, and you don't want to be left in their dust. You want to have fun right now, dangit, and that becomes more important than building a life you can be proud of later.

If you're experiencing F.O.M.O., you may find yourself leaving work, even though you don't quite feel done, because you don't want to miss even one precious moment of a party that will likely last all night. You are unable to maintain a budget for fear that if you skip an expensive dinner with friends, their happy faces on Instagram will induce more jealousy than you can handle. You know not every night out is magic, but you fear that if you miss one, your name will mysteriously go missing from the future invite list. Or worse, your friends will run into Ryan Gosling without you, and he'll be giving out free puppies.

Fear, my friends, is a great motivator. It can cause you to ignore common sense. It can cloud your judgment, forcing you to spend money you don't have just so you'll have a seat at an overpriced dinner table. Reaching your potential means making tough choices that thrust you into unknown territory, and fearing that unknown will hold you back. Yet, being in debt, for whatever reason, isn't as scary to many twentysomethings as missing a social gathering. Debt is like ghosts. Sure, ghosts are frightening, *but* . . . are they even real? However, missing out on a possibly amazing evening out with friends? That is the serial killer *right behind you*! That's the fear that wins, as irrational as it is.

What you should really fear is the lasting evil in your next bank statement or your boss's judgmental gaze when you turn in subpar work, mid-hangover. As you sink into your seat and ask your boss if it's hot in here, consider a change in attitude.

ATTITUDE ADJUSTMENT: Take Time to Develop Yourself

Maybe your life looks good on Instagram, but guess what? It's not good when your life is a mess. There just comes a time when not putting your laundry away is more sad than amusing and bragging about a disinterest in looking out for your own health starts to sound more defensive than fun. The problem here is that you've hinged your happiness on what other people are doing. Ultimately, you fear missing out because you fear who you are when you are alone. Hell, maybe you don't even *know* who you are, which means you are suffering from a lack of personal development. Fulfill yourself independently, and then contribute that "amazingness" right back into your group when, you know, you've got the time and money. After all, people might think your pictures are cool, but they will admire you more if there are things in your life you truly care about, things that you're willing to give up a social gathering or two to achieve. Just be careful to not become obsessed with one goal....

QUARTERLIFE PRO TIP: FACEBOOK IS FOR COVERS

Look at your own Facebook feed. You don't post about the more mundane details of your life, and neither does anybody else; that is why their lives look so fabulous. They're just giving you the highlights! You aren't the only person who has to sit out from time to time. I'm sure there were days Mulder and Scully were just filling out paperwork instead of investigating an X-File about a sewer alien, but that would have been a terribly boring episode.

OUTDATED ATTITUDE: Focusing All of Your Energy on One Passion

Happiness often comes down to balance, so blowing off your life to exclusively chase one passion can be dangerous. After all, it's hard to enjoy success at work if you don't also invest time in friends who want to celebrate it with you. It's kind of like the old MTV show, *My Super Sweet 16*. In it, children from uber-rich families became obsessed with planning their own sixteenth birthday parties, which cost hundreds of thousands of dollars. These children were in the midst of adolescence, when insecurities run rampant, and, because they were so vulnerable, they hinged all of their dreams on the outcome of this crazy party. At the end, as expected, the children always felt let down by reality and spent their super sweet 16 super crying in their green rooms.

Apparently, most twentysomethings learned nothing from this show.

The balance most people experience in their twenties is cluelessly out of whack. The problem is that, like young kids presented with thousands of dollars to plan their own birthday party, a lot of people think building a life is going to be fun. From a young age, you accepted that you'd have to work *hard* to achieve your dreams, but you imagined you'd be working *passionately*, as well. Where is the passion in setting a Google calendar alert to remind yourself to pay rent on time? Where is the excitement in sautéing a healthy assortment of vegetables after a long day of work when all you really want to do is order greasy Chinese food?

Twentysomethings tend to want to focus on the fun part and assume everything else will be forced into place along with it. Maybe you rest all of your hopes and dreams on the outcome of your romantic relationship, giving everything you've got only to discover, in the end, you are left with next to nothing in return. Maybe you bury yourself in your job and assume when you come up for air around age 27, all the health, dating, and friendship issues you ignored will have solved themselves because you'll be a financial success. In reality, coming up for air at 27 turns out to be a lot less glamorous than imagined. Instead of bling, you have all these problems that you've allowed to snowball.

Living a balanced life not only takes planning and dedication but also a real change in attitude that will finally allow you to turn around and face the music. First think: What is your *Super Sweet 16* equivalent? Where are you lacking balance? Once you've decided what you need to work on, read on.

ATTITUDE ADJUSTMENT: Balance Passion with Responsibility and Reality

Don't let pursuing a fantasy backfire on your reality. As great as it feels to be passionate about something and thrust yourself into it like a giddy kid planning a super sweet 16, it's important to keep the rest of your life in balance. The thing about shifting the balance of your life to one activity—one super sweet commitment—is that you aren't just the honored guest at your life party; you are also the cleanup crew. So work passionately, yes, but don't forget that happiness in one aspect of your life doesn't automatically transfer to another. A great boyfriend doesn't translate to a promotion at work or a healthy circulatory system.

In addition, it's important to realize that life, and even happiness, is not all about passion. Sometimes life is just boring. Really friggin' boring. Or frustrating! And that's how it's *supposed* to be. If life gets tedious at times, you're doing it right. Sometimes you have to be supportive and attend your friend's cringe-worthy improv show at a sketchy bar. Sometimes you have to wait inside while your friends take a smoke break because, remember, you quit! It can't all be karaoke nights, snuggling with your boo, and working towards glamorous promotions.

Don't be a spoiled kid who thinks hiring a professional magician is more important to landing friends than being a good listener. You have to be the person you want to be every single day, 98 percent of the day. (I'm giving you a generous 2 percent of the day to eat donuts and shotgun beers.) Being your "best self" takes discipline. You cannot put your life on pause while you focus all your energy on one single thing and, unfortunately, you can't write off bad habits or lapsed ideals as a separate side of yourself. Maintaining balance in your life so you have time to be the person you've always wanted to be means setting boundaries for yourself and others. Sometimes one area of your life will naturally become a priority, but balancing back out should always be the goal. Set up boundaries to keep yourself in check and to make sure you're not letting true fulfillment slide.

TWENTYSOMETHING FACT(ish)

Thomas Jefferson actually began drafting the Declaration of Independence in 1765, at the tender age of 22. However, he got super sidetracked building his dream house. It wasn't until a couple of bloody battles kicked off the Revolutionary War—and confused founding fathers tried to put their fingers on what "inalienable rights" meant—that Thomas Jefferson was like, "Oh crap. I had that written down somewhere!"

OUTDATED ATTITUDE: You're Naive

Let's be honest, twentysomethings can be pretty naive and that naiveté can lead to seemingly endless, misguided decisions. Perhaps you are the type of person who dates men who seem like vulnerable bunnies to you, only to find out they are insecure and determined to drag you down into their rabbit holes. Maybe you told the wrong person at work that you think the boss's white pants and neon green thong are "an interesting choice." Look, it happens, and as you become less naive, you realize that not everyone deserves a place in your life. In fact, trusting the wrong person can set you back for years—mentally, professionally, and even financially. The curse of naiveté can even go beyond trusting the wrong people and extend into ducking responsibility. Because some twentysomethings haven't fully experienced the consequences of playing dumb in the face of crisis, it seems easy to play the victim, reject your role in things, and lose the respect of the people around you. You ignore the bill you got from your doctor claiming you thought insurance would just magically pay it. You get drunk and yell at the guy you are dating in front of his friends and claim it was the booze. When you let these things happen, you also lose the opportunity to learn how to handle those problems with grace. It takes time and an investment in the development of your gut intuitions to finally ditch naiveté and spot disastrous people and situations before they get out of hand.

ATTITUDE ADJUSTMENT: Follow Your Gut

I know. When you are overhauling your life, the most frustrating piece of advice to get is "follow your gut." It seems so vague. But "follow your gut" is really pretty solid advice. It is actually an avenue towards being a stronger, more confident person who learns from her experiences.

I like to think of my gut as the neutral, decision-making territory between my head and heart. My heart's a sucker. My head's a nerd. My gut is just right. It picks up on cues before I've had time to process them. While your brain, heart, and friends debate for months about the merits of the new guy you are dating, your gut probably had it figured out from night one. In fact, your gut is probably the only reason you felt you needed to do so much debating about the topic in the first place; you just instinctively knew something wasn't right.

There is science behind the power of intuition. A study done by the University of Leeds examined a racecar driver who braked before he understood why he was doing it—and ended up narrowly escaping a potentially deadly pileup on the track. "The driver couldn't explain why he felt he should stop, but the urge was much stronger than his desire to win the race," explains Professor Gerard Hodgkinson of the Centre for Organisational Strategy. "The driver underwent forensic analysis by psychologists afterwards, where he was shown a video to mentally relive the event. In hindsight he realized that the crowd, which would have normally been cheering him on, wasn't looking at him coming up to the bend but was looking the other way in a static, frozen way. That was the cue. He didn't consciously process this, but he knew something was wrong and stopped in time."

You've been on this planet for a couple decades, so, by now, like the racecar driver, you know what most situations *should* look like; and when something is off, your gut knots up. Maybe you don't quite know why, but you learn to pay attention. If someone confronts you about a mistake you made and you duck responsibility, your gut knots up, not because you feel guilty for lying, but because you instinctively know that the situation isn't over. Your lie may come back to haunt you.

Take responsibility for your actions and learn from them. Gut instincts are vague at first, but the more you listen, the stronger they'll get. If you have always felt like a pushover, take this to heart. Trusting your instincts is the first step towards feeling strong, so take lemons and make lemonade! Add sugar, though. People always leave that out, but it's an important part of lemonade.

QUARTERLIFE PRO TIP: OWN YOUR MISTAKES

Don't be afraid to take risks. Not risks you would see in Red Bull commercials or ones that might set you back financially, but ones like admitting to your boss that you lied at first, but you are, in fact, the person who jammed the copy machine with construction paper. Call your landlord to say your toilet has been running for three months, and you're sorry you didn't call sooner. Tell your friend you drunkenly told her secret to her enemy. You'll never learn to trust the part of your gut that is trying to make you do the right thing until you have a portfolio of examples proving things turn out for the better when you hold yourself accountable.

NOW FIND YOUR MOTIVATION: THE CATALYST FOR CHANGE

Okay, so now that you know *what* you need to change and *how* you can go about making those changes, it's time to dig deep inside and find your motivation to actually make those changes. You deserve to have a happy, fulfilling life and, as with anything else, success requires motivation. If Hollywood crime dramas have taught us one thing, it's that you can't move forward until you've established motive, right?

If you have been trying to kick bad habits and are failing, it's probably because you haven't found a need to change yet. You need a catalyst to truly commit to that decision. Why do you want to do this? If the fears of continuing to watch your life spin out of control and of never finding true happiness and fulfillment don't get you moving in the right direction, then read on. Here you'll find a few ideas to jumpstart your engine.

A Good, Old-Fashioned Rewards System

If you want to keep yourself motivated, rewarding yourself works. It takes discipline, but it really does work. For example, many health experts recommend approaching your diet with a 90:10 ratio. They suggest that permitting yourself indulgent "cheat" meals 10 percent of the time can actually help you succeed in the long term. Perfection is exhausting. Rewarding yourself every once in a while can help sustain your efforts in the long run—and because you earned the right to indulge by staying focused the rest of the time, you'll be able to truly enjoy your reward without feeling guilty.

Rewarding yourself for implementing change in your life helps to make that change stick. That's because you haven't chucked the things you love entirely; you've reorganized them into your new priorities. We can extend this technique beyond nutrition. For example, if you really want to watch the new episode of *Scandal*, don't let yourself do it until you've worked out or paid bills online. Apply the 90:10 mentality to your time, and earn your leisure.

Responsible Friends

It can also be very motivating to find someone responsible whom you can look up to. As hard as it is to believe, responsible people aren't unicorns—they do not exist in some alternate universe you'll never be able to reach. In your early twenties, responsible people may seem like wizards with special powers that make them highly productive "morning people." However, when you see someone who seems to have it all figured out, take a closer look; they can be your motivation to shake that twentysomething attitude for good. Responsible people are living road maps to your success. True, nobody is perfect, but people who are always trying to achieve higher standards are inspiring people to get to know. Ask questions. Join their book clubs. Ask how they cultivated a career they enjoy and whether it was worth it to grow their own basil (in my experience, no). Sneakily make them your informal mentors.

REAL LIFE SURVIVAL STORY
The Breakfast Club

You can get me to do just about anything if it's presented to me over wine and pizza. That's precisely why my girlfriends were able to talk me into joining The 6 A.M. Wake-Up Club, even though my schedule didn't require that I wake up for work until 8:30 A.M.

You see, we had decided—over wine and pizza, of course!—that we work long hours. At the end of the day we are tired. Working out, answering personal e-mails, pursuing hobbies—these were all things that we wanted to do but felt especially exhausted just thinking about after a long day of work. So after adding a cheese plate to our order, we decided to start waking up at 6 A.M. I thought this idea was brilliant and assumed we would all, as a team, forget this idea the minute the clock struck no-more-pizza.

Then, at 6 A.M. Monday morning, I got a group text. "Good morning!" it read. You see, that's the thing about responsible friends. They keep *you* responsible. So I got up and got more done in those two-and-a-half hours before work than I had gotten done the entire week before. It was pure magic. By the end of the week, I was the one initiating the texts. Having friends holding me accountable kept me motivated. The best part was that my evenings were then reserved for relaxation or socializing without other responsibilities hanging over my head.

My friends and I have been getting up at 6 A.M. for two years now, and we're still going strong. And, to make it even better, we regularly celebrate the success of The 6 A.M. Wake-Up Club with—you guessed it—wine and pizza!

Explore Your Interests

As we've discussed, ducking responsibility results in the feeling that your life is spinning out of control. The best motivation for taking that control back and achieving your goals is understanding what *you* want. Once you feel your needs being met, you'll want to keep pushing for it. So, what do you want? Well, you may need to explore a little bit to figure it out. Here are some ways to go about it.

Take a Class!

Taking classes for fun is . . . fun! You don't have to worry about your grade point average like you did with those fuddy-duddies back in high school. Plus, you get to dabble in that thing you always told yourself you'd dabble in before your actual career took over. If you aren't sure what kind of class you want to take, think back to something you loved as a kid. Maybe not all the way back to when you wanted to train monkeys for the circus, but back to when you wanted to write a screenplay or build a robot. Instead of making sense of the world by trying to fit in with peers, find an outlet for your energy and creativity by testing your boundaries and trying something that's outside your daily routine.

Do Things Alone

Go out to dinner alone. Take that class alone. Volunteer at a soup kitchen alone. Be friendly to a stranger. Oftentimes, interacting with the world, outside the confines of who you've decided you are around your friends, builds confidence. It also helps you make decisions that please *you* rather than having to defer to a group mentality or compromise. Just don't spend too much time drinking alone. That leads to a lot of problems, not least of which is online shopping while intoxicated.

Be Inspired by Entertainment

I stand by *Friends* reruns. Always. But sometimes you need to use the time you spend consuming media to open new avenues in your mind. Perhaps you usually read nonfiction biographies—then branching out to a fantastic science fiction novel might be good for you. Maybe you usually select a romantic comedy on Netflix. Try a documentary instead. Explore new interests for yourself, and the world will feel bigger. The bigger the world feels, the less power things like F.O.M.O. and work anxiety will have over you.

Change Your Surroundings

Sometimes you need to get away to rediscover where you belong. After all, it's easy to lose your sense of self and long-term goals when you are essentially living the same day over again. That's how habits, good and bad, are formed. Stepping out of your comfort zone—whether it's to visit a museum for a day or lie on a beach for a week—can help you to reevaluate. Jessica de Bloom, a researcher at Radboud University in the Netherlands, analyzed research on stress around the world and published her conclusions in the *Journal of Occupational Health*. She found that people who take vacation or frequently escape to more relaxing surroundings often find more meaning in life and have more energy—energy you can invest in getting your life together! The best way to do this is to rope in your best friend to split the cost and entertain you with her delightful company. Best friends are always down. Those suckers!

QUARTERLIFE PRO TIP: WHERE TO GO TO FIND YOURSELF

- Closet Nerds—Go to Comic Con. Bring your favorite T-shirt.
- Lapsed Hippies—Find a mountain and hike, my man.
- Lost Jocks—Hustle over to a Hoop It Up tournament or Warrior Dash.
- Disheveled Preppy—Work it on a beach where manicures are most appreciated.
- Thirsty Bookworm—Find a city and research the hell out of it before scheduling the stops you'll make while touring.
- Lonely Party People—Go to New Orleans. I hear the strangers are friendly.

REAL LIFE SURVIVAL STORY
"Girl-cation"

When my friends Megan and Lisa turned 27, they were exhausted. Their dating lives were failing, their jobs were draining—the whole deal. They saw pictures of Palm Springs, California, on a blog and decided to spend the next few months saving so they could make an escape. They were like those cartoon mice that see a picture of Paris on a cheese wrapper and hang it up in their little holes for inspiration.

When they got there, Palm Springs was everything they'd hoped for. In New York, their clothes were trendy but confining. In Palm Springs, they stuck to sports bras and sneakers. They were more comfortable and liberated than ever. Their conversations in the desert revolved mostly around what they *wanted* and not just how things already *were*. Being away gave them space to dream.

Back in New York, they pushed each other to keep changing their surroundings. They rearranged their apartments. They organized makeup-free picnics in the great outdoors instead of high-maintenance bar nights. They did things like hike and gave themselves permission to eat lunch away from their desks every so often. They attended free, local events—like one at the library hosted by drag queens who made over patrons to look like children's book characters. When you see unfamiliar areas of life or the country or even just the city you live in, it makes the trappings of your own life feel much less confining.

Go Big or Go Home

Motivation to go after the life you want tends to snowball as your confidence builds. The more you allow yourself to shake up your routine, the more you'll realize it's not so bad. And should you ever lose your way, well, allow me to motivate you. . . .

If you're like the majority of people out there, you've made a New Year's resolution. And yes, these resolutions can be annoying. You get yourself excited about your goal, only to discover that you're not the only one. You hit the gym and find every machine is taken. The locker room is so full that people inevitably bump butts. Suddenly, your fear of failing increases simply because you can sense the collective fear of failure in that stinky, bleach-y air.

Yet, even though it feels pointless, make a resolution. Even if you feel doomed to fail, do it all year long. Any day you think of something you wish you were doing, start that resolution immediately, and try your hardest to keep it. Don't relegate your clumsy efforts to New Year's—fail literally, all year long!

But remember; you will also succeed! Not always! But it happens! The best resolutions are dramatic ones. A lot of people will encourage you to start small. Just make one small change, they say, like eating breakfast. Eventually, your healthy eating habits will begin to snowball, and your bigger goal will be achieved! But, sometimes small changes are bullshit. Sorry, small changes, but I'm calling you out!

You should "Go big or go home." Resolve to work out more *and* eat healthier *and* read more books! Why ease in? Why hang on to a status quo you aren't happy with? Small changes inevitably become small priorities. Big changes become challenges; would you be more excited and proud to climb a mountain or a molehill?

You know where you've gone wrong in the past. You know you've been naive and fearful and lacking in focus when it comes to the day-to-day details of being your ideal self. So find your motivation, and hit the ground running. Being a happy and fulfilled adult is something you deserve.

And don't be afraid to tell everyone your resolutions. Go ahead; be smug and brag like you've already achieved it. You have to put yourself at risk of being made fun of if you fail. You know, that whole "people holding you accountable" thing.

Yet, if you don't keep up your goal of working out four times a week or can't stop yourself from watching *The Real Housewives of Garbagetown*, don't be so hard on yourself. That's counterproductive to the movement! If you fail—if you bump butts, inhale the stink of strangers, and eventually quit—simply set a new goal. That's just how it goes. Maybe next time, instead of the gym, you'll give yoga a whirl or hire a personal trainer. You aren't a failure; you just need to find another way to make your goals work in the framework of your life. Ask yourself: Are there reasonable sacrifices you can make to attain success and fulfillment? Is there a balance you need to find to help you persevere? None of this is out of your control. Put in the effort to customize a path that is right for you, and then do not live in fear of falling short; just adjust and keep moving.

THINGS TO REMEMBER

Before you can start busting up ruts, you have to try to understand them. You can't beat your problems until you take a critical eye to them. It's like how in the movie *Independence Day*, they couldn't blow up all the aliens until Jeff Goldblum figured out how to upload Windows '95, or whatever, onto the mother ship. That's what we did in this chapter; we examined the mother ship. As you move forward and figure out how to make room for the changes you've identified, remember:

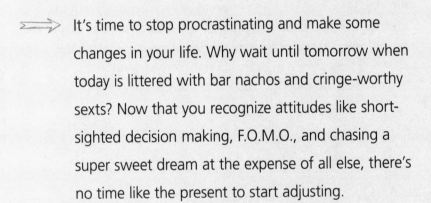 It's time to stop procrastinating and make some changes in your life. Why wait until tomorrow when today is littered with bar nachos and cringe-worthy sexts? Now that you recognize attitudes like short-sighted decision making, F.O.M.O., and chasing a super sweet dream at the expense of all else, there's no time like the present to start adjusting.

Adjusting your attitude can be accomplished by setting boundaries and taking some time to think about what you want, not just how you fit into a group or how your daily routine fits into a status message. The key to fulfillment is balance in your life—balance between finding who you are, relationships, work, and health.

⟹ Find your catalyst for change. We all know how hard it is to get started on change. Motivation can come from anywhere, including something as simple as taking a class, changing your surroundings, or following a good example. As simple as it is, nothing can be accomplished until you find that fire.

⟹ Go big! Don't be afraid to really go for it. Small changes inevitably become small priorities, so really push yourself. Do not go quietly into the night . . . this is your Independence Day!

CHAPTER 2

Strategy: Making Space in Your Life to Get It Together

Now that you understand your situation a little better and have found your motivation, you have to make room in your life for new and better habits. But, of course, the hardest part about starting a new routine is finding the time and energy for a new routine. In this chapter, you'll learn how to clear up your time—whether it's using a planner or leaving happy hour a little early—and tricks to mentally keep yourself moving in the right direction, towards the fulfilling life on the other side of your twenties, even when external frustrations threaten your concentration.

CLEARING TIME FOR REACHING GOALS

I'll bet you and everyone you know are "super busy." It is nuts. Maybe you feel as though there isn't enough time to do what you actually want to do, like you are being dragged from one mundane commitment to the next. There just doesn't seem to be enough time in the day to get your life in order! But organizing your life doesn't have to feel like an all-out war. A day is what you make of it, and sometimes making the time to change your life is a simple matter of reprioritizing. And once you've reprioritized, it's a matter of actually handling those top priorities, even when you'd rather ignore them and look the other way to the direction of your couch, TV, and some guacamole. This section will walk you through clearing your time and then actually holding yourself accountable for using that time. So stop procrastinating, and get ready to take a look at some sneaky time wasters. And speaking of procrastination, yeah, it's on the list.

Identify Sneaky Time Wasters

It's easy to spot the obvious ways you are wasting your time: Facebook, television, Animal Crossing, etc. Yet, if you take a closer look at your habits, I bet you'll find some hours that are simply unaccounted for—Bermuda Triangle–size holes in your life. What were you doing? Were you abducted by aliens? Aliens who made you stalk your ex on Facebook for three hours?

I won't make you rule out aliens just yet; I'm not a *total* buzz kill, but allow me to present a few other activities that are likely filling those mystery blocks of your time. You'll also learn some tactics you can use to shut these and, really, any time wasters down before they (not to be dramatic or anything) *destroy you.*

Hitting Snooze

Some mornings, you have enough time to put together a pretty amazing work outfit. Other mornings, you hit snooze for an hour and rush out the door in a jean shirt, jean pants, and brown boots. It makes you look like a cowgirl, *and* it makes the whole day feel frantic. Instead of trying to fit in a few extra minutes of sleep in the A.M., try to get enough sleep at night. And here's the thing: That extra snooze sleep is not great sleep. There is no REM cycle involved. So, embrace a regular bedtime, the same bedtime every day. It's worth it!

Surfing the Internet at Work

A 2012 survey by *Salary.com* found that 64 percent of employees visit non-work-related websites every day at work. Of that group, 39 percent spend one hour or less per week, 29 percent spend two hours per week, 21 percent waste five hours per week, and only 3 percent said they waste ten hours or more doing non-work-related activities. I'd say it's a safe bet that those numbers are underestimated.

If you feel like you're losing your days to the corporate grind, consider logging out of all social media at work and ban your favorite blogs and websites from your "favorites." While you may think you are just taking a mental break, surfing the Internet at work breaks up your work flow and slows you down—or stops you dead in your tracks. Plus, not everything you see online is a *fun* break; sometimes it's a low bank balance or a frustrating political debate between Twitter friends. When you do get back to the task you are being paid to do, you're forced to waste time clearing your head and refocusing. As the end of the day approaches, you'll feel rushed if you've wasted time or maybe you'll just end up having to stay late to make that time up. So cut the Internet nonsense and get out of work as soon as you can. Reading a frustrating political debate will be much less alluring once it's clear you're forfeiting personal time better spent . . . *not* reading a frustrating political debate.

Online Shopping

This should be a time saver, but if your guard is down, the Bermuda Triangle will close in. You may spend an entire Sunday surfing for the perfect sundress, then end up hastily buying a pair of leopard print shorts at two in the morning. You just want to buy something after all that time! Instead, shop online casually when you are not hell-bent on some holy-grail item you aren't even sure exists yet. A lot of sites allow you to create a list of favorites that you can easily order later or just reorder without having to delve into the abyss of endless online inventory. Stay focused and Godspeed.

QUARTERLIFE PRO TIP: AVOIDING ONLINE SHOPPING BINGES

Think of e-mail from your favorite online stores as tentacles from a beast trying to pull you back into its lair. Every once in a while, designate an "unsubscribe day." On this day, don't just delete these e-mails; unsubscribe from their list. This will keep you from getting pulled in on a day when you feel weak.

Having One More Drink

Leaving a party is hard. (Remember F.O.M.O. in Chapter 1?) Twentysomethings have a tendency to turn a pleasantly early night out into a game of chicken. The first person to go home must survive a peer gauntlet on his way to the exit. "Past your bedtime?" "Lame," friends chastise. Oh, the humanity! Instead of ordering one more drink in the hopes that a mundane night is about to get cray up in here—don't. Let it go. Go home. You may end up paying interest on that drink in the form of a hangover. Have you ever tried doing the same workout with and without a hangover? You'll find you are about half as capable. Jumping rope? More like, "jumping? Uh . . . Nope!" Repeat after me: "A hangover is only worth your time if karaoke's involved."

Skipping Nights Out with Friends

A common thing to do when you are feeling suffocated by your schedule is to start canceling plans with friends. Cutting yourself off from humanity feels like the only logical thing to do. After all, if you're feeling stressed, you might as well feel desperately alone, as well, right? Wrong! Make sure you save time for a few, great, intimate get-togethers. They are an important investment of time. Friends feed your soul, which, in turn, helps you avoid a multitude of time wasters—Facebook stalking, sulking due to F.O.M.O., etc. It's a good idea to go home and be productive, or work out or get some sleep, sure; but being a straight-up hermit is depressing. People like you, believe it or not. They miss you. You need a hug.

Now, it's true that you can't always be productive and downtime is important. However, these sneaky time wasters tend to overstay their welcome and eat up time that is better spent becoming your best self. Now that you've banished these activities from your life—in dramatic fashion, I hope—the next step is organizing the time you've cleared up using every good habit's best friend: a planner.

QUARTERLIFE PRO TIP: DON'T BE AN EX-STALKER

Stalking an ex on Facebook can become a dark hole where time stands still and emotions run amuck. To stay above ground, block your exes from your newsfeed. For good measure, every time you find yourself typing his or her name into a search engine, immediately stand up, walk away from your computer, and put your nose against a wall like a kid in time-out. You're in time-out, twentysomething!

Get a Planner to Organize Your Newfound Time

Everyone loves a to-do list. They are like ice cream. Kids can't get enough. I, personally, like buying a weekly Moleskine planner at the beginning of every year and keeping it on me at all times. I just like physically putting the pen to paper—but if you like using your phone, do it! Don't let me stop you!

Now, if you buy a planner and find yourself poring over it doing anything that can be described as "meticulous" or "thoughtful," then you are doing it wrong. A planner is for jotting, not plotting. All you should be doing is opening it up, jotting down your reminder, and then putting it away. You should never look at a planner for more than 30 seconds on any given day. Trust me, though! Those 30 seconds will do wonders for organizing your life. They'll help you place everything you need to know into one place so that things don't fall off your radar and snowball into bigger problems later. Bigger problems like late fees, conflicting plans, and forgetting to send out the invite to your friend's birthday until the only people who can show up are a random selection of acquaintances and you . . . but only until 9:00 P.M. because you double booked the evening. Don't be this frazzled person. Instead, try to keep track of the following things in your planner.

TWENTYSOMETHING FACT(ish)

In 1976, at the tender age of 21, Bill Gates kept his to-do list on a computer the size of a modern day dresser. He insisted it was the wave of the future, and his friends were like, "Whaaaaaaat?"

Plan Your Shopping List

Everyone hates running out of things, and, with a planner, you will never again realize at the worst possible time that you are out of toilet paper. Never again will you be standing in the shower with wet hair when you realize you forgot to buy more shampoo. Gone are the days when you're halfway through a peanut butter sandwich before remembering you're out of milk. A world with fewer surprise stress parties can be yours! When you notice your supply of something is low, pull out your planner and jot it down. Then, it's as simple as getting into the habit of glancing at your planner every time you shop. Bonus points if you get so far ahead that your bathroom cabinet looks like Walgreens's toiletry aisle. Replace the replacements like a baller (or like a Walgreens employee).

QUARTERLIFE PRO TIP: JOT DOWN YOUR SPLURGE FANTASY ITEMS

Listen, I'm cool. Planners don't have to be stuffy. There's no reason your planner can't also store your hopes and dreams! Go ahead and add "fabulous fall boots" to your shopping list. If you remind yourself of the splurge items you actually want, it will keep you focused next time you shop for yourself. This will help you cut back on those last minute purchases that lead only to regret.

Plan Your Cash Flow

Ever forgotten about an auto-pay bill and ended up overdrawing your account? It's heartbreaking. With a planner, the minute you set your account to auto-pay a bill, just jot a reminder to double check that the money is still there the day before your payment. You can also write down when you're owed money. I'm not saying get picky every time a friend owes you five bucks (although, don't think I forgot LINDSY!); but if, for example, your cable company says they'll be sending you a refund check, no matter how small, get off the phone, and immediately write in the next week of your planner, "Has cable company sent money yet?" This reminds you to follow up. Every time you squeeze a penny out of a giant conglomerate, an angel gets its wings.

Keep Your Workout Log

Keep track of your activities so you'll have evidence that you worked out . . . or did not work out. It's hard to keep track otherwise. You don't have to schedule every workout days in advance. Instead, your planner will help you know if it's been a while and you need to restructure your free time for a workout.

Mark Down Big Work Deadlines

Because you probably spend all day thinking about work, it's tempting to feel like you already have that schedule figured out, but, because your social life can bleed into your work life, and vice versa, it helps to keep those schedules in one place. If you have a big deadline coming up next month, write it down in your planner so you remember not to schedule social gatherings or dentist appointments during the time, if you can help it. Then, you can also be sure to schedule a night out to blow off steam right after that deadline passes.

Plan Your Social Calendar

If you do this right, you won't have to log in to Facebook to know your social schedule ever again. When someone invites you somewhere, whether they send you a text, an e-mail, or a Facebook invite, write it in your planner immediately. You need that info in one place. If you begin to see your week fill up and it's stressing you out, start turning down plans. Take back your time!

Make your planner the blueprint for building the life you want. Keep it updated and close by. There is only one problem with a planner—it's not a drill sergeant. If you are tired, it is not going to get in your face and make you do anything. What happens when you've streamlined your time, organized it into a planner, and yet still can't find the energy to follow through on your goals and responsibilities? Read on....

Get Things Done Even When You Are So Tired

The last step in taking full advantage of your time is doing the best you can to cut out the urge to procrastinate. Webster's dictionary defines procrastination as, "instead of going for a run, spending 45 minutes reading about Liza Minnelli on Wikipedia for some reason." Procrastination is most common when you just don't have the energy, physically or mentally, to feel confidence in your ability to perform a task. There are two main factors that lead people to delay their goals in favor of wasting time.

1.   They are afraid of failure. Their goals are exciting to think about, but they are afraid if they actually go for it, they will fall short.
2.   Shifting gears to do something that requires effort is hard.

These two kinds of negative thinking can stop your progress towards a balanced adult life. Conveniently enough, there are two main ways to fix these problems.

Stay Positive

You *can* achieve the career you want, the health you need, and the relationships you deserve *if* you can keep negative self-talk to a minimum. Feeling intimidated by the idea of failure is natural, but don't let your insecurities bully you into complacent procrastination and, essentially, ignoring all of your problems.

If you're not sure how to kick that negative energy to the curb, you first need to understand that your insecurities are not based in fact. Though they sometimes feel overwhelming, your insecurities do not actually eclipse your talents. Consider this: The human brain has evolved to have a negativity bias that causes you to pay more attention to negative emotions than positive ones. This made sense for primitive humans. They lived in the wilderness naked, so understandably they became obsessed with protecting themselves from perceived threats. Their senses became attuned to negative thinking for their own safety. But in today's overstimulating, wooly mammoth–free world, that preference for negativity is less necessary and can actually make your problems seem much bigger than they are.

The good news is that you can rewire your brain. Studies have shown that the more you practice positive thinking, the stronger those positive paths in your brain will become. With effort, positive thinking can become second nature and help you feel less intimidated by your goals and the world around you, which will, in turn, make you less likely to procrastinate and more likely to get things done. Here are some exercises to strengthen the positive paths in your brain. They may seem simple, but they work!

- **Count your blessings:** Every night, take note of three good things that happened to you that day. This is your mental workout routine. In an emergency case of the "Mondays," when you notice you're starting to dwell and feel especially emo inside, count your blessings immediately, and you'll do a mental 180.

- **Use positive talk:** Make less small talk about the weather and more small talk about something funny you saw on a blog—or just show interest in someone else's life instead of the rain. Breaking a mundane habit like cursing the weather won't motivate you to make life changes, but positive small talk can get you off on the right foot.

- **Acknowledge when someone has done something well by telling them:** Start with the goal of giving out one compliment a day, and soon they'll come naturally and probably more often. This will increase your ability to see good things in the world, as opposed to focusing on the negative.

- **Listen to happier music:** Ever notice how you could be having a perfectly fine day until Phil Collins's "Against All Odds" comes on and brings you to tears? Listening to the latest, upbeat Beyoncé single can do the same in reverse.

- **Introduce yoga and meditation into your routine:** An important part of yoga and meditation is clearing your mind. When you clear your mind, you'll find you also clear out all that negativity those cave-dwelling ancestors left behind and leave room for positivity to come back in.

With positive thinking firmly in place helping you to fight procrastination and fear of failure, the next question is what to do when you have to get it together, but you'd rather just sit down. When expending effort is the last thing you want to do, the best tactic is to use momentum.

Use Momentum

Momentum is the reason a five-ton semi-truck can't stop on a dime. It's the reason one home run can inspire a losing team to charge forward and win the game—and it's the reason you can get shit done, even when you think you are too tired. Whether it's physical or mental, momentum is on your side when you want to fight procrastination.

The trick to using physical momentum to combat procrastination is to avoid your couch when you want to get something done. It's seriously that easy. If you've just gotten home from work, you are still on your feet, and momentum is on your side. Think of your couch as a brick wall threatening to crash your semi-truck and put you out of commission for the evening. If you want to make a healthy dinner, ignore the couch, and head to the stove. If you want to work out, flip that couch the bird, and put on your running shoes before you ever sit down. You may feel as if your body is possessed as you robotically lace up your Nikes, your mind pleading with you to flop down on the couch for just two minutes, but don't give in. Just keep on moving—*away* from the couch.

Mental momentum is a little bit harder to gather but well worth the effort. It's much easier if you've been practicing your positive thinking because you're going to have to dig deep for all of the reasons you've been wanting to achieve a particular task and use the combined force of those thoughts to move you forward towards your goal. Want to be the kind of gal who washes her dishes right after every meal? First, eat your last forkful of peas. Next, turn on that "You're The Best" song from *The Karate Kid* montage. (Okay, this step is optional, but why *wouldn't* you turn it on?) Now, think about the sink that inspired all this—a friend's clean sink that you admired a couple of weeks ago. Remember how disappointed you were in yourself a morning after *not* washing your dishes. (Did you maybe find a cockroach in there? That helps the momentum for sure.) Think about how you'll still be able to watch TV while you soap up a pan; how smug and adult you'll feel knowing some silly college student is watching the same show while lying motionless on his futon, dirty dishes out there for everyone to see. Take all of these thoughts you've had regarding clean sinks during the last few weeks and throw them towards the sink with such momentum you can't help but grab a sponge and *get it done*. You'll be surprised at how easy this is to do if you can just get your mind wrapped around it.

REAL LIFE SURVIVAL STORY
The Human Energizer Bunny

I've done some research on human Energizer Bunnies. You know, people who always seem to be productive? My research has consisted of, conveniently enough, shadowing my friend, Max.

In college, Max used to show up to my parties, turn on his iPod playlist, and start to dance, no matter how subdued the crowd. And, strangely enough, his enthusiasm always rubbed off on people, and dance parties ensued. Post-college, he never stopped going big and had his dream job as a national, big-deal music correspondent by age 28. The man has met Gwen Stefani at this point—yes, *the* Gwen Stefani.

Max has always just looked a little bored with trash-talking and complaining. He recognizes that, if given an inch, negativity will take a mile. He sees every action he takes as a springboard into something else. He doesn't just attend a party; he attends a party and talks to everyone in the room, even the famous ones. He figures he's made it this far, why not go one step farther and meet some cool, new people? It's a bold way to live and it's led him straight to his dreams.

The difference between people who procrastinate and people who achieve their goals is their ability to harness positive thinking and momentum. But you aren't born one way or the other; these behaviors can be learned and become habit. Yet, if you feel like you are constantly faking that positivity, you may need to take some time to figure out where your head is. All is not lost—mental space can be organized, too.

UNCLUTTER YOUR MENTAL SPACE AKA THE FUN PART

There is a time to be productive and barrel through even the most miserable of tasks that you want no part of (bra shopping, am I right?), and then there is a time to balance all that hard work out with some time for reflection. Keeping your mental baggage light is important. You have to protect yourself from overstimulation, which can lead you to ignore the issues that bother you and stand in the way of complete fulfillment. You have to find ways to keep the turmoil in your mind to a minimum—everything, from getting a good night's rest to having the strength to brush aside your anxiety and face your overdrawn bank account, hangs in the balance. You're pretty much stuck with your brain 24/7, so you have to make sure it works for you.

In your early twenties, you may have felt that you needed alcohol and lots of friends—or at least Netflix—to relax. But now you probably realize that all of those activities were just a way to shut down your brain, silencing it with substances or noise. The thing is, you can't just keep hiding the clutter. If you don't keep your mental closet tidy, soon that mess will come busting through the doors, and you may lash out unfairly at people you love. Fortunately, there are a few different ways that you can deal with your mental baggage head-on.

Give Yourself Permission to Enjoy Some Quiet Time

Read a magazine, enjoy the sun, paint your toenails—do all those things quietly or by yourself. Making the most of your time doesn't always mean checking things off your to-do list or living it up with your friends. An important part of being centered is spending time with yourself without any set task or expectations holding you back. So give yourself permission to be alone with your thoughts and pamper yourself. The more room you give your mind to ponder, the more the issues you have in life will seem to solve themselves. You just have to give yourself some time to think and appreciate your place on this tiny speck of dust we call Earth. You know, let your inner hippie take over.

If you can find room in your budget to put some actual miles between you and your problems for a week, here are some bonus points to score on the ideal vacation.

- Don't panic, and spend 20 hours frantically prepping at the office the day before you leave.
- Pack only comfortable shoes.
- Go to bed super early, and wake up for sunrise.
- Do not check your e-mail or post anything online.
- Talk to a stranger about his day (in a safe, public setting, fool).

The nice thing about getting to know yourself is that it helps you build confidence in your point of view. Which is great because sometimes expressing that point of view is your key to inner peace.

Say What Is on Your Mind, Even When It's Not Pleasant

If you're like most twentysomethings, you may feel as though you don't have a lot of time to be difficult or angry. After all, you've just started to figure life out. You feel pressure to forgive as soon as possible so everyone can move on and still have fun at the party!

Here's the thing—whether you acknowledge it or not, anger hangs out. It festers. The only way to resolve it is with forgiveness, and forgiveness isn't just divine; it is earned. I'm not saying the other person needs to earn your forgiveness. I'm saying you have to find a way to forgive others, whether they are seeking your forgiveness or not. The hard part is that it takes practice to let yourself be angry without letting it take control. Anger is something you have to take the time to process at your own pace, and it can't be rushed.

Taking a shortcut to forgiveness is easier when you are young. You have the promise of graduation around the corner. Or you'll just find a new job. Or you'll move and make new friends. But your twenties are about building something real. You can't keep running; you have to start appreciating and cultivating what you have. The best way to do that is to turn and make nice with your anger. Here are some things to keep in mind as you learn how to really forgive:

Anger Is Meant to Protect You

Anger can make you feel irrational, yes, but it isn't irrational by nature. It's a very real reaction to being wronged. It keeps you from rolling over and taking it from people. Instead, you feel this rush of energy to stand up for yourself. Before you act on or ignore anger, examine it. Figure out what you're reacting to and what it is you need to set straight. It's best to do this contemplating far from the face you want to bitch slap to oblivion.

Be Careful Where You Point Your Anger

You can spend a lot of years ignoring anger only to discover that you've been pointing it at yourself the whole time. This happens to a lot of twentysomethings. Someone took credit for your idea at work? You get mad at yourself for letting her. A guy didn't call you back? You get mad at yourself for not being the woman of his dreams. Anger is potent, and, if you're not careful, it can tear you apart. If you continue to be angry with yourself, it's only a matter of time before your anger overflows onto the next-easiest target—people you love. So next time you are beating yourself up, try to identify what is really making you angry. You need to figure out whom and how to forgive; otherwise unprocessed anger will make you bitter.

Anger Lingers

Anger stays with you like New Year's Eve glitter. Everyone has dealt with anger, so they will understand. Once you've examined your anger and said your piece, it might still be hanging around. You know you can't keep harping on it without being unfair to the person who made you mad, yet the anger is still there hanging out. This is frustrating, but anger tends to burn at its own pace, so you just have to accept it. Think of it like your new pet lion, and get comfortable with it; don't ignore it. Would you turn your back on a lion? Of course not! You wouldn't unleash it on people, either, because that would be cruel. Just let its presence keep people in line until one day you realize the people who deserve your company have stayed in line naturally and your lion has sauntered away.

Anger Is Serious Business

According to the Mayo Clinic, "research suggests that inappropriately expressing anger—such as keeping anger pent up, seething with rage, or having violent outbursts—can be harmful to your health. Such responses might aggravate chronic pain or lead to sleep difficulties or digestive problems. There's even some evidence that stress and hostility related to anger can lead to heart disease and heart attack." So, in other words, anger is serious business, guys. Wear a pants suit and bring your "A" game. The more you express your needs when it matters, the less anxiety and pain you'll suffer when you're on your own.

REAL LIFE SURVIVAL STORY
The Unambiguous Silent Treatment

A friend of mine once found out her new boyfriend betrayed her trust. Unbeknownst to her, he had been secretly hanging out, one-on-one, with his ex-girlfriend in what he says was an attempt to seek closure. When my friend found out, she was angry. Why hadn't he just told her? It was early in their relationship, and he didn't want to upset her; but it still felt suspicious, and my friend felt betrayed. Yet, as understandably angry as she was, she didn't want to break up. This seemed like something they could work through. She just needed time to process her anger. She explained this to her boyfriend and calmly proceeded to not talk to him for a few days. It was the silent treatment, but there was no guesswork involved; he knew exactly why she wasn't talking to him. He was sad but gave her space.

I was impressed. In my experience, anger within a relationship had usually come down to an immediate fight and a race to reconciliation, sometimes feeling so rushed that I still had anger left over. I'd try to ignore that anger in the spirit of love but couldn't help but beat that dead horse long after I had promised to forgive. It wasn't healthy! It was maddening for all involved! My friend was inspiring to me.

Every morning during her silent treatment, we talked through her anger. Was it still there? Was her head clear enough yet to have a big talk with her boyfriend about it? Her boyfriend did a lot of thinking during this time, as well. After a few days, when my friend was ready to talk, he was very receptive to her feelings. He respected her anger and, while he wanted her forgiveness, understood that it'd be selfish for him to rush her. They successfully moved on because they were honest—more honest than if they had prioritized reconciliation over truly understanding each other. Everybody deals with anger differently, but my friend taught me to slow down to my own pace and make sure it's truly resolved.

See a Therapist If You're Struggling

Sometimes ruts come with regrets and baggage that you can't quite get out of your brain. Many twentysomethings just find getting older to be overwhelming, and they feel depressed even though they don't know why. Sometimes the last step in turning over a new leaf is admitting you need professional help. There is no shame in this!

If you're interested in seeing someone, call your insurance company and figure out your coverage. Often, employers offer employee assistance programs that will refer you to a therapist and offer a limited amount of sessions for free so you can decide if this is the right person for you. If you don't have insurance, many universities offer affordable sessions to area residents.

While most people find therapy helpful, many also find it to be quite different from what they expected. Here are a few myths to bust before you begin the process.

- **Therapy is not like talking to a friend:** Your friends support you no matter what because they love you. When they tell it to you straight, it's a big deal because it doesn't happen often. Therapists, on the other hand, have insight the average person doesn't, and though you may just want them to affirm everything you say, that is not their job. They are there to guide you to new and helpful realizations.
- **You won't feel better right away:** In order for therapy to work, you have to be an active participant. You can't hold back and should try to think about your therapist's insights and how they apply to your life between sessions. You're unpacking your mental closet here. It's messy for a few sessions, at least, so get ready to feel a little torn up. A good therapist will know when to pull back so you won't feel overwhelmed and can manage your emotions after you walk out the door.
- **Therapy isn't always a cry-fest:** Some days you will walk into therapy without anything to say that is worth crying about. It doesn't mean you should cancel your next appointment immediately. Maybe you've worked through what you needed to, or maybe you're just in a good mood for the day. Talk to your therapist before you decide you are "cured."
- **You're allowed to break up with your therapist:** You have to feel comfortable, and sometimes it just doesn't work out. Ask a few questions on the phone before your first session to see how you feel about different therapists. Find out their area of expertise to see if they match up with your needs,

and assess your chemistry over the phone. You may talk to quite a few therapists before you find the right one.

The more effort you put in to understanding yourself—what stresses you out, makes you angry, makes you happy—the more confidence you'll have to make the right choices. Finding the time and energy to make change in your life will help you get in shape, out of debt, and even get a promotion, sure; but, most importantly, it will help you think about your own needs and fill you with the confidence you need to become a successful and fulfilled adult.

THINGS TO REMEMBER

In this chapter, you've learned at least one big lesson; if you're going to break bad habits, you can't just want to bust ruts— you've got to fall in love with busting ruts. Busting ruts has to be your new boyfriend. You've got to make time for him and make room, both mentally and physically. As you move forward and work to change your life, one step at a time, remember:

 Change won't stick unless you organize your time to truly make it a part of your life. Crush sneaky time wasters like having "one" more drink, hitting snooze, and spending too much time on the Internet at work by logging out of social media, going to bed earlier, and going home if the night doesn't take a dramatically exciting turn by drink two.

 Get a planner! Record everything you do so you have a visual representation of how you are spending your time and money. It'll help you clock your own habits, both bad and good, and adjust.

Embracing positivity and momentum is your key to beating the urge to procrastinate. Practice positive thinking as if it is an exercise by reflecting on the day's positive experiences before falling asleep, meditating, and listening to upbeat music.

 It's important to get into the right mindset if you want to change your habits. You must unclutter your mental space and become a master of relaxation. Go to therapy when you feel you've hit a wall with rut-busting, and let go of anger at your own pace. Don't feel rushed.

PART 2

MOVE FORWARD WITH THE PLAN TO GET IT TOGETHER

By now you've found time in your schedule for getting it together. Hopefully, you've even found some motivation. Most likely, your motivation comes from within, but if someone is paying you cold, hard cash, even better.

Now, it's time to start moving forward. In this part, you'll take a look at the specific ruts you may have gotten yourself into (stagnant career, poor health, debt, lame relationships), and you'll learn some specific ways to kick their ass and make being a fearless, successful adult look easy.

Turn on "Eye of the Tiger." Listen to it on repeat for the remainder of this book.

CHAPTER 3

Make Your Career Work It for You

After years of education and planning for your career, it is surprisingly easy to feel ill-prepared for that very career. Asking for a raise? Finding a good work-to-life ratio? You've heard about these things, but putting them into practice probably seems a little overwhelming. And you may have heard people *talk* about office politics, but you've also heard people talk about the jungle. You probably don't feel ready to fend off an attacking jaguar, and there's a good chance you don't feel comfortable leveraging for a promotion—even if you've earned it.

The thing is, nobody is going to ask you what you want out of your career. If you want something at work, you have to speak up. Twentysomethings have a tendency to take energy that should be spent climbing the ladder and, instead, expend it on career jealousy, complaining, and petty gossip. In this chapter, you'll learn how to break free from the negativity and how to take control of (even advance!) your career. How do you get the powers that be on board with your advancement? How do you know this is the path that will make you happy? How do you make sure you're being compensated competitively? You'll find the answers to all this and more in this chapter.

You spend nearly a third of your life at work; this chapter would like to help you enjoy it. Loving your career, even being *okay* with your career, can go a long way towards fulfillment and success in all aspects of your life. So, don't take this career stuff lightly. You have to work towards a career you care about, but first you have to climb out of some all-too-common career ruts.

EARLY CAREER RUTS

When you first enter the world of adult careers, you're bound to make a lot of mistakes. It's natural. You know that dream where you show up to work only to realize you've forgotten to put on pants? Well, these early career ruts will make you wish your biggest problem had been forgetting to wear pants. At least that little snafu would have gotten a good laugh, and you'd have been home by dinner!

There are the usual bad days, which you can't control, and then there are those unhealthy work habits you settle into, almost as if you can't see them, until one day you realize you're miserable. You're probably familiar with those habits—prioritizing work over life, unconstructive complaining, and petty gossiping. In fact, it's common for twentysomethings to rely on them in misguided attempts to make their points of view known. The thing is, these are bad ways to communicate. As consuming as these habits may seem, don't let them rule your career. Let's take a closer look at how you can untangle these ruts from your success and start making sure your voice is heard.

Your Poor Work-to-Life Ratio

Right out of school, most twentysomethings kick off their careers by working themselves to the bone—a misguided attempt to show the boss their dedication. You do this, in part, because things don't come as naturally to you yet as they do to your more senior coworkers, and you want to impress your boss. Yes, you have to put in the time to learn, and that might mean a few late nights at the office; but skipping the gym, neglecting doctor appointments, and constantly ditching your friends to work late takes this dedication too far. It might clear time for work, but it catches up to you later. Maybe you'll pay your dues, but you'll feel too burned out to want to advance much farther. It's difficult to fully enjoy a successful career without a fulfilled life on the outside. It's called work/life balance and you'll need it in order to maintain a level head while on the job, calibrate your focus to see your goals beyond the next dead-line, and, most importantly, not be a jerk. Here are some additional signs that you've taken your obsession with work too far.

- You eat your lunch after it has gotten cold because you had to answer just one more e-mail. At this point, you've forgotten that French fries are served warm.
- At yoga class, when everyone is dedicating their practice to someone they love, you dedicate it to your boss in hopes of a promotion. Namaste.
- While on vacation, you pay money out-of-pocket to get in-flight Internet so you can check work e-mail.
- You feel your position threatened by everything that moves in the office. You're jealous of fans that oscillate.
- Your friends love you completely but, literally, just forget to invite you places anymore.

While you want to showcase your good work ethic, if you keep saying yes to work that is killing you, you essentially project a false image of yourself that is not sustainable. Instead of giving your boss reasonable expectations, you've set yourself up for failure. In the end, this is poor communication. You want your boss to know you're building your career and that you are in it for the long haul, not that you are at risk of becoming burned out. If you're stuck in this career rut, stop it. A healthy work-to-life ratio is worth fighting for and, in general, having a fulfilling personal life makes you a better coworker. You'll be more upbeat, inclusive, and open-minded once you've established that you don't live and die by this job. Sometimes answers, be it a creative breakthrough or the key to a quicker workflow, are right in front of you if you allow yourself to take a step back, instead of spinning your wheels with your nose to the grindstone. So how do you take a step back?

Get a Full Night's Rest

Just because you're making enough time for your workload by cutting out sleep, doesn't mean that time will be quality. Studies have shown time and time again that people make poor decisions when tired. Driving tired can be as bad as driving drunk. Sleep deprivation is also a wrecking ball to your health. Do you want to go through life as a zombie person? They have terrible skin! So how do you commit yourself to a full night of sleep?

- **Adopt the mantra, "Work is a bottomless pit."** Thinking this way sounds dark, but it stops you from telling yourself you could accomplish *everything* if only you weren't a human being with the physiological need to sleep. *Your work is a bottomless pit.* Which means you can pick it back up tomorrow. For tonight, relax, sleep, and keep your work-to-life ratio intact.

- **Unplug from technology an hour before bed.** Do this even if you think you need to look over something work-related during your "unwind" time. Research has shown that the constant stimulation of technology makes it harder for you to focus and shut out irrelevant information. Imagine what this does to your ability to relax and fall into a sound sleep. Instead of work or Internet, focus on getting yourself into a clear mental space for a good night of sleep. Nothing is worse than going to bed agitated, and then having the boss come to you with tentacle arms in the middle of an otherwise lovely dream.

- **Make sleep a priority.** Do a well rested trial run during which you prioritize eight hours of sleep a night for one week, no matter what. You may find that your lack of sleep was slowing you down, and, with more sleep, you're still able to get the same amount done but in less time.

When it comes to finding balance between work and life, sleep is a good place to start. Making time for sleep will keep you thinking clearly. If you feel you need to work more hours, don't take it out on a good night's rest. For goodness' sake, twentysomething, sleep is on *your* side.

Keep Your Friends

To maintain a healthy work-to-life ratio, don't reduce your personal life to just coworkers. It's natural to start to feel a strong kinship with your coworkers—you guys are going through so many of the same things—but beware . . . your work-to-life balance could be getting out of whack. It's important to make an effort to maintain outside friendships, so try to see non-coworkers once every couple weeks. Your friends are your friends for a reason. They're (hopefully) supportive, unbiased people who will catch you when you feel frustrated at work. If you don't have someone outside of your coworkers to vent to, there's a good chance you will lack an outlet and become bitter. If you don't make an effort, you are damaging these friendships, and you'll miss them when they are gone. Guaranteed!

In addition to hanging out with the people you actually care about, make an effort to shift your social life away from the office by following a few simple rules.

- **Call your mother:** She gave birth to you. All she asks in return are periodic updates on your life so she can brag to her friends. Stop breaking her heart! And call your father sometimes, too. He's hurt that you always just ask for your mother when he answers.
- **Do not hook up with your coworkers:** Talk about getting your balance out of whack! It's not even about your

reputation at work, though being the office make-out bandit surely has its drawbacks. It's about finding balance in your life and becoming a fulfilled adult. Work is tough enough given the distractions in the rest of your life, so do you really want one of those distractions to walk by your cube every day? Do you want to hear about that distraction's new girlfriend right before a big meeting? Do you want to overthink it when that distraction doesn't ask you to go for coffee at the usual time you get coffee? Of course not!

Remember, part of being a well-rounded employee is having a well-rounded life. Being efficient and staying Zen are appealing characteristics to employers. So make sure you are efficient by getting your rest and reducing distractions like secret office romances. Stay Zen by finding outlets for work stress that have nothing at all to do with work. If you don't find those outlets, you'll end up being the office whiner, which is yet another early career rut.

TWENTYSOMETHING FACT(ish)

A whopping 87 percent of twentysomethings who have hooked up with a coworker lie in bed at night cursing the names of Jim and Pam from *The Office*.

You Don't Focus on Long-Term Goals

Another career rut that twentysomethings get stuck in is not focusing on their long-term goals. Yes, it's really easy to lose sight of these goals given the massive amount of work already on your plate, but you need to keep your future plans in the back of your mind. Maybe never telling the boss "no" and accepting more work seems to help you climb the ladder, but, when you reach a certain level, it'll do nothing but weigh you down. Focus is key. Let your long-term goals motivate you, and push aside the need for positive reinforcement right now. Yes, sometimes you don't have a choice, and you have to take on extra work that doesn't quite fit into your five-year plan. But, as you take it, you should recognize that extra work for what it is—paying your dues. Suck it up when you're the newbie, but if the ratio of "dues" paid to long-term career building continues to feel unbalanced, ask yourself what you are expecting to gain out of this job and if it's a step towards where you want to be. If you think this job can get you to the next level, don't just take on the work as it comes—be proactive and start creating the next opportunity for yourself. Here's how:

- **Learn the job you want, even if nobody has offered to teach you yet.** Get nosy. Ask questions. Plan ahead to stay late for a couple of nights so that you are not cancelling plans, but keeping your life balance in mind as you add hours to your week. Use this extra work time to write up an idea you have so you can get feedback and learn from your seniors.
- **Keep your boss and senior colleagues in the loop about your progress.** That way, when you raise your hand to be a part of the next big project or take on more responsibility, they'll know you've been preparing and are more likely to

trust you with the work. Be patient. They may not call on you right away, but keep trying to put your hat in the ring.

- **Talk to your boss about cutting back on certain entry-level duties to make room for a step forward.** This will help you maintain a healthy work-to-life ratio and stop you from burning out before you finally get the job you've been gunning for. Pick which duties you'd like to shed before having the conversation. That way, your boss won't take away something you love doing. For example, if you work in a chocolate factory, for God's sake don't forfeit the chocolate-covered bacon account!

If you focus on the long term, it helps you to remember that you are trying to build and sustain a life, not burn out. Considering how your day-to-day tasks are fitting into your overall career plan will help you to prioritize them realistically. If you've already proven yourself on a certain task dozens of times over, let someone else take it on this time—you have a whole, wonderful, outside life to maintain.

QUARTERLIFE PRO TIP: DON'T FEAR THE INTERNS

It's scary to let go of entry-level duties for fear that you'll fall short as you attempt to climb the ladder. You may worry about becoming obsolete, so you keep trying to do it all—living in constant fear that if you leave for one hour, an intern will be doing your job by the time you get back. But don't fear them. Interns and employees below you in the office hierarchy are on your team. Give them opportunities you've outgrown. Your relationship is symbiotic, and you must grow together. If all goes well, they'll soon be at your level, and you'll have a trusted teammate.

Complaining

After working yourself to the bone, to the point that you have no personal life, you might find yourself feeling under appreciated. Fair enough! But after all of your hard work, do you want your most recognizable contribution to the team to be negativity? Negativity in most work environments is a virus that spreads quickly, and complaining won't do anything but annoy your coworkers and drag down office morale. So set a positive and constructive tone—be a leader. After all, leading is not just about giving orders—it's about boosting morale.

A lot of people would just plain tell you to "Quit your bitching," but I want you to take the time to consider why you are slipping into the role as the office "Debbie Downer." Are you just feeling under appreciated or are there legitimate issues you think need to be fixed? If you are under appreciated, you should instead try to make your good work noticed by scheduling time to review your job performance with a superior. If you see issues with the way things are done, you should help everyone by suggesting alternatives. Complaining muffles the message you are actually trying to send and is usually just a negative spin on a situation that, in reality, has positive fixes. So. Here are some ideas to find that positive spin so you can finally quit your bitching!

Keep It Positive!

Stop yourself when you are about to say something negative and, instead, phrase it in a positive or constructive way. Suggest a solution. Instead of saying, "Sally doesn't know how to do her job," say, "Next time, I will be especially specific when I request things from Sally until she gets the hang of things." Instead of saying,

"My boss hasn't responded to my pitch because he doesn't appreciate me," say, "I'm going to send a quick follow-up e-mail about my pitch." Not only will this keep you thinking positively, but it will also actually bring you to actionable solutions you may otherwise have overlooked while complaining.

Don't Martyr Yourself

If you think you work harder than everyone else, odds are you've unwittingly cast yourself as the "office martyr." You know the office martyr. She's the person who always acts overwhelmed and unhappy, yet never seems to take any steps towards reducing her workload to a manageable level. Chances are she's never taken you up on an offer to grab lunch together but has, instead, used your invite as a chance to highlight how she'll be toiling while you customize your burrito bowl at Chipotle. Extra guac, hold the tiny violins, please! Everyone sees right through that person, and I've got news for you—people don't exactly love 'em. Everyone loves the "person who works hard by day and who doesn't make me feel guilty for wanting to eat dinner with my family at night . . . and who sometimes brings in donut holes," not the ones who behave as if they are being victimized by Scrooge on Christmas Eve. Realize that you aren't alone and you aren't actually working harder than everyone else. Don't think of yourself as being against your coworkers. Like it or not, you suckers are connected. If you want everyone to get on your page and work efficiently so you can go home and watch *The Voice*, you have to work together. Inquire about other people's workloads, sympathize when they are overwhelmed, don't try to one-up them, and always ask for help if you are drowning in work. Let others know you value their input and are committed to working efficiently.

TWENTYSOMETHING FACT(ish)

Researchers have uncovered a correlation between a parrot imitating a hyena and the person who accepts an extra assignment and then melodramatically tells his coworkers how swamped he is—they are equally annoying.

Vent to Your Friends

If you have to complain, be sure to complain to friends who have nothing to do with work. Remember how we went over the need to invest in relationships with non-coworkers? This is one small reason why! Friends that have no investment in your office life can help you chill out and stop sweating the small things. To them, your serious work issues are like *Seventeen* magazine–style, "Traumarama" stories. Your boss is scary to you but ridiculous to them. That's a good thing!

Get a New Job

If you truly dislike your job so much that you have nothing nice to say, begin the hunt for a new job. Do something about your misery. You should not only have a healthy work-to-life balance but you should also have a healthy perspective on the role one job plays in the grand scheme of your career. If you've stopped complaining and have been constructive and things haven't gotten better at work, treat the job you have as a paycheck and mentally start to move on. Moving forward goes a long way towards feeling positive about your lot in life. And if you decide to call it quits, be sure to leave on good terms. We'll discuss this in more detail later on in this chapter, but know that burning bridges always comes back to haunt you.

Keep in mind that everyone has work complaints that well up inside like a volcano, but you need to be aware of where you erupt. Make your complaints constructive, look out for the welfare of your team, and talk to uninvolved friends when you need to blow off steam. If all else fails and nothing can be fixed, don't be afraid to start looking for a new job. If you hit the point where you are looking elsewhere, make sure you are focused on what you want and not comparing your success to that of your peers. That is another early career rut that will stand in your way.

QUARTERLIFE PRO TIP: FIND A CAREER MENTOR

School can teach you only a drop in the bucket of what you'll need to know for a real career, which is why mentors are so important. Many big companies offer official mentoring programs, but reaching out to someone you work with or simply admire can have the same effect. Most people, at all levels of their careers, love talking about themselves. It's flattering when someone is willing to listen. Just approach them humbly and without expectation. If you're "goin' places," helping you makes *them* look good. Really, you're doing them the favor (don't say that out loud).

Coveting Thy Neighbor's Career with Jealousy

Whether it's your coworker or just an old classmate you stalk on Facebook, comparing your career path to a peer's can mess with your head. Finding idols, competitors, and mentors can be a great thing, and these people can be great motivators; but there is a difference between finding inspiration and feeding self-doubt. For example, while a mentor may inspire you to network with someone who knows of a job opening in your field, comparing yourself to someone may lead you to believe you have no right networking because you don't have the skills when compared to that person. Or maybe you see someone in a different field of work all together and worry that you chose the wrong path entirely, causing you to lose enthusiasm for your goals. Letting the accomplishments of others feed your self-doubt stops you from taking risks that are absolutely vital to furthering your career. Here are a few concepts to keep in mind on your path to letting go of the jealousy and insecurity other people's careers sometimes bring up in you. These are concepts you can remind yourself of when you are feeling weak and they can stop you from window-shopping outside someone else's life. After all, your life is pretty good as it is—and if you continue to focus on your goals without beating yourself up with negativity, it will only get better.

They Worked Hard to Get There

Bummed that people in finance have enough money to roll around in, while you break down in thankful tears upon finding an extra five bucks in your jeans? Well, let it go. You didn't want to do their job, and that's why you went another way. Recognize that you are admiring their lifestyle but need to take into account the reality of their day-to-day struggles. Try, instead, to see the results of their personal hard work as all the more reason to focus on your own goals. And if you simply would rather not work as hard as they did—and would instead like to focus on family or maxin' and relaxin' in a fiscally responsible way—then remind yourself that you are cultivating an envy-worthy lifestyle in a different way. Everyone makes sacrifices, even happy people—the thing that makes them different is accepting that balance between their work and personal life.

Let Talented People Inspire You

Some people actually are legitimately more talented than you, and that's okay. Use their successes to inspire you to do better! If talented people make you feel bad about yourself and you feel that you can't look to them for inspiration, well, that attitude is your problem, not theirs . . . and it does not bode well for your career. Think of it this way: Should an Olympic sprinter try to catch the person ahead of her in the race and embrace the spirit of competition to become a better athlete? Or should she stop and cry about it? The answer is pretty obvious. Of course she should be competitive and try to catch up! If you feel that you just want to sit down and cry, then that's a confidence issue, and you can't give in to it. Ain't nobody got time for that.

Trust Your Struggle

Trust your struggle—*your own* struggle. You are going to face challenges that are uniquely tailored to you. Don't you feel special? Your struggle can be anything from debt to illness to an inability to sing on key. The bottom line is, you can't compare yourself to someone else. It's apples to oranges! Your coworkers may not have your weaknesses, but they also don't have your strengths. Maybe your particular set of skills and interests will slowly push you towards different achievements from theirs. Wouldn't it be a shame if you ignored your own strengths and instead struggled in someone else's shadow? For example, stand-up comedian Louis C.K. was once a writer for *Late Night with Conan O'Brien*. While they were only four years apart in age, it was more than a decade before Louis C.K. achieved the household-name level of success Conan O'Brien had in the same field. Yet, they each put trust in their own specific brand of humor. Trying to rush into something that isn't a fit for you only keeps you from reaching your full potential. A goal to match someone else's success is empty; a goal to meet your own potential is fulfilling. So look at your abilities, cultivate them, and use them. If you nurture the skills at your disposal, one day some young twentysomething will be envying *your* career.

The bottom line is that being inspired by the success of others is healthy; feeling like a failure in their shadow is counterproductive. Stay focused on your own goals. Have confidence in the career decisions you've made that led you to where you are. Your career is a marathon, and you aren't running it alone, so use the pacing of your peers as inspiration; but also trust that, if you stay focused on your own potential, you will finish the race proudly as a success—and then you can go get a cheeseburger. Don't feel threatened by those around you to the point that it makes you feel insecure; and, if you do feel threatened, keep your mouth shut about it. Office gossip is another career rut to look out for—it is an uncontrollable animal that bites back. . . .

Office Gossip

Another career rut you may have fallen into on your track to success is the lure of office gossip. Many people gossip in a misguided attempt to bond. You want to feel like part of the inner circle but may really be communicating that you are untrustworthy. The funny thing about gossiping is how intimate it feels while you are doing it with a coworker. Picture it! You talk for a while about small things—casual things—just to gauge each other's trustworthiness. The drinks keep coming as the cadence of your conversation quickens excitedly. It's as if you agree about everything! Then suddenly the tone shifts. The charge forward stops abruptly. You're holding back.

"Oh God, I shouldn't say this!" you burst.

"Well now you *have* to," someone counters. Which isn't true; you don't have to say it.

But you do! You spill your guts! From there, the secrets just keep flowing, trading back and forth. You can't believe how much you and your coworker trust each other! It feels just a little wrong, but you can't stop! These secrets are a bond! It's hard to explain, but it's as if these words are binding you for life! True friends forever!

Cut to the next day when some schmuck you hardly know recites one of your deep office secrets back at you like he's got an inside scoop, a secret that you trusted *someone* not to repeat.

Everyone understands completely where the urge to gossip and trash-talk comes from. It can be super fun and full of laughs! Everyone feels insecure from time to time with their job performance, so it sometimes feels good to target other people. It calms your own insecurities. It is a tempting rut to fall into. But stay strong; I've got some reasons you shouldn't gossip at all. Does that not entice you?

All right, gossip head, let me try this again: I shouldn't tell you this but . . . ah, hell, here are some reasons you shouldn't gossip at all!

Gossip Is Seedy

The world of office gossip and trash talk has a seedy underbelly. While it feels therapeutic in the moment, these conversations come with strings attached, and those strings connect directly to your work hierarchy. You may find yourself removed from projects you enjoy just because you've trash-talked another member of the team—not because your target has found out but because the person you confided in thinks she is doing you a favor. In other words, you talked the talk, and now you've gotta walk the walk. It is a stifling walk. It is like walking in the desert, I'd imagine. I've never done it, but movies make the heat look very stifling.

Gossip Turns You Into a Hypocrite

If you become the office gossip, there's a good chance you'll end up feeling like a hypocrite. If you want forgiveness when *you* accidentally show up to work without pants on, you have to build that karma when your coworker does it. And, really, would you say these things to the face of the person you are saying them about? Is your intent to hurt people? Probably not. Sometimes blowing off steam is necessary, but the more you do it, the more you compromise your integrity and become the type of person *other* people gossip about. You probably won't enjoy gossip so much when that happens. Ay, there's the rub!

Abstaining Turns You Into a Superhero

If you are known as a vault, you'll find yourself holding all the valuable insider information. If you seem like the dependable person who rises above all things petty, people will come to you when they have actual concerns. You'll be *The Keeper of Secrets*! Live it up. That title makes you sound like a superhero. Invest in a cape. You earned it. This ability to control yourself when faced with juicy information is the difference between entry level and being on your way to the career you truly want; it's the difference between amateur and pro. The more you practice discipline, the more confidence you'll have that you deserve success and fulfillment.

TWENTYSOMETHING FACT(ish)

For any work issue you have, there is a Buzzfeed link that will not only sum it up for you but also offer comprehensive solutions using only *Sister, Sister* gifs.

You Need to Focus on Problem Solving

Every job out there can be summed up in two words: problem solving. More often than not, gossip allows a problem to fester instead of solving it. So stay positive; don't indulge in negative or petty things like gossip. They are wasted energy. Stay focused on the work and cooperation. If you have an issue with someone, work up the nerve to talk to him about it directly so you can both put the problem behind you. In the end, being known as a trash talker hurts your reputation as someone who can be counted on to solve problems efficiently. It's key to maintain a positive attitude. Eyes on the prize; you've got a job to do!

The bottom line is that, if you want to be taken seriously at work, you need to seriously resist the gossip. Relegate your gossip to friends who are uninvolved. Coworkers are less likely to trust your judgment if it seems as though you are motivated by petty drama. So be the office vault, and rise above these temptations. Once you've cleared gossip and drama out of your head, it's easier to focus on what it is you want out of this job—building your career and climbing the ladder.

BUILD YOUR CAREER ALREADY

Getting through your quarterlife crisis is really about taking control of your life so you can become your definition of fulfilled. For your career, it means facing the fear that you're in the wrong field or simply aren't good enough to be a success in the long run. In order to tackle these issues, you have to explore the opportunities in front of you and create new ones for yourself as you start to get a feel for what's working. Passively soul-searching is important, but most of your answers will come from actively engaging in trial and error.

Getting started, you'll make a lot of mistakes. Learn from them, and then make new ones; but there comes a point in your career when you've learned pretty much everything you need to know to start moving on up the ladder. It's not brain surgery. . . . Well, unless you're trying to become a brain surgeon! But even then, it's not rocket science. . . . You've got questions, sure, but you can just sense it's time to rise past the middle and get that position you've been eyeing for years. You know, a position that doesn't feel transitional, something you could settle into for a while. For example, maybe you want to move up from an assistant to a manager, from something that would be considered entry-level to something that requires experience. The steps towards building your career share a lot of the same mentality as kicking career ruts. That is no coincidence because the biggest rut of all is letting your career stagnate. There are a few main steps to focus on when you are trying to move forward.

Put Your Eggs in a Variety of Baskets

You've heard the phrase, "Don't put all your eggs in one basket," right? You know why they say that? Well, if you only have one basket full of eggs and you drop it by mistake or because you are tired of that basket, you don't have eggs anymore. Just a mess of shattered dreams . . . I mean eggs. Well, you can take the lessons you've learned lugging around eggs and apply them to work. You see, until you have the experience you need to center the job you want in your crosshairs, it's important to keep exploring other options.

Most companies, as a rule, expect you to stay happily in an entry-level job for two years. After that, it's time to start pushing forward. If the ladder seems backed up at your current job, make sure you keep your resume fresh and submit it elsewhere. It's important not to stagnate; you need to keep developing your skills and moving forward. Take classes, start projects, and meet regularly with friends to keep each other up to date on your progress. After all, it's not healthy to feel like one job can shatter your whole world, so care enough about yourself to build a life full of interests to fall back on. Remember that whole work-life balance? Well, it's really important to have when you're building your career. If you have a bad day, it's nice to leave the office and know that your job does not define you or your entire career. You've got Harry Potter fan fiction to write (or, you know, whatever your other basket is).

Put Yourself Out There

If the ladder at your current job seems like it's got some room, start climbing your way up. As you do this, remember that, no matter how hard you work, nobody can read your mind. Your bosses may love your work ethic, but that doesn't mean they're going to offer to help you realize your dreams. They probably don't even completely understand what your dreams are—unless you tell them! So, once you've established that you are reliable, the next step is seeing if you can count on them to help hoist you into your next role. As we've discussed—you should think long term and consult with coworkers about what *they've* done to achieve the success *you* want. Once you've organized what you want and started taking on those responsibilities, arrange a meeting with your boss and use that time to explain what you've been doing and how that will play into your long-term goals. What projects would you like on your plate? You have to do the legwork so your manager can get on board.

REAL LIFE SURVIVAL STORY
Don't Ask, Just Do

I currently write and edit trailers for television shows. But long before I worked my way onto the creative team, my job description relegated me to shipping VHS tapes back and forth. I was awesome at that. I was an all-star. But those skills weren't going to get me any creative meetings; that would involve jumping to another department. I had to redirect my path. On my own time, I started bringing unsolicited scripts to creative directors so they could critique me and help me grow. I set aside a few hours a week to cut trailers that nobody asked me to work on. My enthusiasm impressed the creative team, and they started reaching out to see if I had anything else to show them. Then one day, I broke through. I received my first assignment to actually air on television—a trailer for a very violent horror movie!

Between you and me, I hate horror movies. This was the opportunity I'd been working for, and it was also my nightmare. But you have to work your way up from somewhere, so I did it. I watched that movie backwards and forwards to make sure I turned in the best piece I could. Well, I watched it backwards, mostly, so that I'd know what horrors were coming before they gave me a heart attack and/or nightmares. I also muted it. But the important thing is I got through it. And now I have enough clout to flat out refuse those kinds of projects all together.

Use Leverage to Get That Promotion

Sometimes, even after you've made it clear what you want, your official promotion can get backed up in the HR department. At this point, as time crawls forward, the opportunity to leverage may arise. Let's say you've paid your dues, and now everyone knows you are gunning for a promotion. You've been meeting with bosses and going above and beyond for months but haven't received a promotion-commitment in return. Well, because you didn't put all your eggs in one basket, another company, impressed with your interview skills, has offered to hoist you up the ladder before your current employer. Of course, you can't choose which company to grow your career with until you have all the information. It's time for you to leverage.

Asking your current employer to fast track your promotion because you have another offer on the table is tough territory. It's generally frowned upon if you haven't put in your two years of dues-paying. It's especially frowned upon if you haven't made it clear that you have goals your current employer wasn't helping you to meet. But if you've done everything right, and you've found yourself with another job offer, don't freak out. First, pat yourself on the back for finally having options after toiling away. Then, tell your current employer there is another offer, and calmly let them know what it would take to get you to stay. Do you want a promotion, more money, better benefits? Lay it all out in the same meeting in which you bring up that you've got another offer. Make sure they know you want to stay. Negotiations can get messy when they are rushed, and odds are, with the other employer waiting in the wings, they are going to be rushed. Here are a few tips to help you make sure you have all the information you need when you have two options to choose from.

- **Don't Bluff:** Don't leverage too hard with a job you don't actually want to take. Your current employer might call your bluff. If you get a job offer you already know you are not interested in and end up turning it down after you've tried and failed to leverage, you've made it clear to your employers that you are desperate and willing to twist their arms for no reason. They don't like that. The other option should always be more appealing to you than if your current job remains stagnant. Don't think of yourself as forcing your employer; rather, think of yourself as gathering information because of an offer you can't ignore.

- **Use Your Power:** That said, don't allow your current employer to scramble to put together a counteroffer you won't actually consider. That's bad business karma. If you want the other job, leave without leveraging. If you want more money from your new job, try asking upfront without using your current job to force their hand. *They* want *you,* so use that power.
- **Don't Give Too Much Away:** There is no rule saying you have to tell your current employer what you are being offered elsewhere. Give them the number and title you *want* and leave it at that.
- **Stick to Your Deadlines:** Make sure you give your possible new employer an exact deadline for when you will be accepting or rejecting their offer. Stick to it. Don't burn that bridge!
- **Stay Stone Cold:** Don't get emotional mid-leverage and start airing all your grievances. That might lose you any counteroffer. Try not to be threatening in a professional setting. Who are you? Gordon Gekko?
- **Remain Committed:** If leveraging works, and you stay at your current job, don't keep job hunting. You now must remain committed to where you are for a while, ya animal!

Even if you put all your chips on the table, your current job may not be able to fast track your promotion for HR reasons. If this happens, you can either leave or accept that they will promote you in the near future. After all, if they never intended on promoting you, they'd let you go. But if you're staying put for promises, get those promises in writing, and ask about an immediate salary bump as a show of goodwill. A salary bump will be easier for your boss to get approved quickly through HR than a title change.

Ask for a Raise

Listen. You've made a name for yourself. You've been getting it together. You've been working smart, prioritizing what's on your plate, and improving morale with your can-do attitude. It's time you asked for a raise. Unless you ask for a raise from time to time, you'll probably be paid less than an employee who comes in from the outside. A raise will keep you competitive in your field's talent pool as well as help your savings account finally cross the $20 mark.

Do you sometimes doubt whether you deserve a raise or feel as though you are a fraud about to be discovered? Rest easy, my friend; pretty much everyone feels that way! The trick to getting past this insecurity when you want a raise is getting your ducks in a row before you head in so you have concrete things to build your confidence. These are the ducks you'll want to consider lining up.

Start Dressing Up for Work

When you want to fill a role that requires experience, it's time to start dressing for the job you want. The best way to highlight how indispensible you are to the company is to start dressing like you've got an interview elsewhere. Especially if you work in an environment where you are able to dress somewhat casual most days. When the bosses see you dressing nice, their interviewee alarms will go off, and they'll remember how indispensible you are. You don't have to whip out a pants suit, but a pencil skirt or blazer every now and then should do the trick. To be clear, this isn't a "get sexy" initiative. Just look nice.

Chronicle Your Accomplishments

Many twentysomethings have the tendency to undersell themselves. Perhaps you worry you'll seem too cocky otherwise. But just like your boss doesn't know your dreams until you tell her, she won't know your accomplishments, either. She needs to be reminded. Pretend you are updating your boss on a project; give the details factually and without framing them in emotion. Don't sound whiny or censor yourself in an attempt to appear humble when money is on the line. Just state the facts. I'm a big fan of visual aids to help guide you. When it comes to asking for a raise, sliding a list of your accomplishments across the table to your boss is clutch. Yes, you do have to *literally* spell it out for them. Make sure to describe the accomplishments on the list in ways that make it clear you've gone above and beyond your job description. If you can quantify things, like the amount of money you've saved the company, even better; feel free to be that specific. This is your moment to prove to your bosses how organized, responsible, and detail-oriented you can be—just the kind of employee they want to keep happy with a raise. Focus on yourself here; don't focus on what you are doing compared to your coworkers. Your success isn't relative; this is all about you.

Just Ask, Already!

Don't even waste one second fantasizing about the perfect moment to ask. Every time I'm working on a project that I think will knock everybody's socks off, I fantasize about strutting into my boss's office when all is said and done and demanding a raise. Preferably, I do this as confetti rains down around me. The thing is, usually another project comes up right away. There is no time for celebration. Or, because I'm a perfectionist, I'll see one minor flaw and decide to ask after my *next* big project. You know, after I've *really* proven myself. The thing is, if you are proving yourself every day, you can feel it. There is no exactly perfect, fairytale moment. If you feel like you've been doing good work, it's been well over a year since your last pay increase, and the company is in a relatively good financial space to provide a raise, then *that* is the moment to ask. Don't let insecurity hold you back, and don't let perfection be the enemy of the good.

Use Positive Language

When you ask for a raise, it's a good idea to change up your language—both verbal and body language. You want to present yourself confidently so that your bosses know you are the kind of employee who is capable and reliable—someone who doesn't require the micromanaging that comes with people who always second-guess themselves. Don't say, "I feel like my project was a success." Cut out the "I feel" opener and confidently say, "My project was a success." Don't say you "tried" to do something, say you "took the initiative" to do it. This may feel awkward and unnatural, but plow through and be sure to smile; otherwise you'll look like a possum in headlights.

Keep yourself from body language that closes you off, like folding your arms and not making eye contact. Avoid motions that people subconsciously associate with lying, such as fidgeting and tensing up your body. Instead, immerse yourself in positivity. Don't just smile with your mouth, smile with your eyes. Or as Tyra Banks calls it: Smize.

Get Someone on Your Side

Talk to your immediate boss or manager before going to HR or the head of your department. Get someone with power on your side. They should speak on your behalf, separately, in addition to helping you prepare for the ultimate raise discussion you'll be having with whoever controls the purse strings. They'll probably have some more specific pointers for you on how to get what you want out of the specific environment you are in. You need an advocate—a witness to your reliability. It also helps to show you respect the chain of command and are not the kind of employee who goes over people's heads.

As you go through the process of getting a raise, remember that it involves quality work and your confidence in that quality work. Let yourself have swagger. Double up on your positive thinking exercises as you prepare to meet with your boss. Like with anything else, the key is thinking positively. This is true even when you decide to part ways with your job.

Always Leave on Good Terms

If you decide to quit your job, don't forget—the time you put in at that job and with those people is still a tool you can continue to use while building your career. That job is still a platform that will help elevate you farther out of your career rut, no matter how sick you were of it when you decided to leave. Being a truly fulfilled adult means making life transitions with grace and without regret. There's no reset button on life, and the next chapter is probably still going to have the same characters so continue to cultivate everything you have and leave every job with your head held high. Work your full two weeks' notice with a smile on your face, if you can.

You should never go to bed or leave a job angry. If you leave, leave because you crave a new experience, not to get revenge on the boss you've been complaining about. You'll almost certainly find things to hate at your next job, too, so it's best to let bygones be bygones with the devil you know. Most industries are small. You will see this boss again—probably in Hell but also at work functions. Who knows? You might even end up back with the same company in a few years. So don't tell off your boss. Watch *Jerry Maguire* if you want to scratch that itch. Never slam a door behind you. Sure, every time a door closes a window opens, but let's be real—doors are easier to walk through. Windows are how you split your pants.

THINGS TO REMEMBER

Maneuvering your way into a successful career isn't just about book smarts; it requires a certain amount of street smarts—well, I guess this is more like "water-cooler smarts." You must acknowledge your own strengths and weaknesses while maintaining a positive attitude for the benefit of office morale. In the midst of your quarterlife crisis, you'll realize you've learned quite a bit. The next step is actually applying those lessons to moving forward so that your life can grow beyond cold French fries and fearing your boss to fresh bacon cheeseburgers and collaborating with inspiring peers.

⇒ Fight for a balanced work-to-life ratio. It is the only way to maintain an accurate perspective on what you want. Protect healthy habits like sleep, nutrition, and friendships outside of work. Don't be a scrooge!

⇒ Avoid counterproductive behavior that will drag down your positive attitude. Don't complain; offer solutions. Don't gossip; be a vault. Don't let yourself become jealous or insecure when you look at the successes of your peers; understand that you are on your own path to success and they are on theirs.

⟹ Don't be shy; build your career! Let people know what your goals are, enlist mentors, and work towards the title you want. Everyone feels like an unprepared fraud sometimes, but don't let your insecurities stop you.

⟹ Ask for a raise every couple of years, even if you aren't ready for a new title. Your value has increased with your experience. Employers would do well to heed Beyoncé's warning—if they like it then they better put a raise on it.

⟹ If you leave your job, leave on a good note. You have enough exes to hide from in the grocery store; don't add your old bosses to that list.

CHAPTER 4

Your Body Is a Temple, Not a Hoarder House

Once you've stopped working yourself into an early grave, what's next? Well, I didn't want to tell you this back when work was stressing you out and your only source of happiness was M&M's but . . . next comes giving up M&M's.

As you age, you'll start to notice your metabolism slowing down. It creeps up on you like a child from one of those Japanese horror movies. First, your hangovers start to last longer, damaging your productivity the next day. Then you can't order a side of fries without a side of bloat, and wearing a belt becomes a regrettable decision after you eat lunch. You just feel achy and uncomfortable in your own skin. Next thing you know, you feel lethargic. This lethargy makes all of your adult responsibilities—from doing your laundry to your taxes—feel like climbing Mount Everest. You think you just need coffee, but after a while you realize it's more than that. Your days of joking about how little you work out are over. It's time to save your metabolism! It's time to think twice (or thrice!) about your health!

Except . . .

Health can be intimidating. Sometimes it feels like a specialty interest, like knitting or alpaca farming. It seems fun and all, but you're not sure you have time to learn all there is to know. You ask yourself things like: "Does climbing the stairs to my apartment count as a workout?" "What is the new super fruit?" "Are egg yolks healthy again?" "Am I pooping enough?" You probably took health and physical education classes in school, but most likely all you learned was that the food pyramid is mostly bread and teenage boys like whipping balls at each other.

Health is vital to living, so don't write it off as a specialty interest. Sure, there are health-related decisions that require a lot of research or consulting a physician—running a marathon, going on a cleanse, going vegan, etc. However, there's no need to be drastic or train in every new health fad. There are basic habits you can begin immediately to make health a normal part of everyday life. In this chapter, we'll keep it simple. We'll break down the basics of health insurance (Hint: less WebMD, more accurate MDs). Then, you'll learn about what's fueling your body and take a look at the easiest ways to maximize nutrition (Hint: less beer, more broccoli). Then you'll get the inside scoop on the mechanics of your body and how to keep your muscles moving before they rust (Hint: less sitting, more listening to Jillian Michaels). But first, you'll need to let go of an idea so intimidating it's probably been holding you back . . . the perfect body.

IT CAN'T ALL BE ABOUT BODY IMAGE

Let's get one thing straight! There is no such thing as the perfect body. In the '90s, magazines pushed you to be stick thin and then the '00s were all about the ass. Chasing the perfect body is a complete waste of time, and, when you ultimately fail to reach the mirage, it'll kill your drive to truly succeed. By putting emphasis on body shape and the way you *look*, you're going about self-love all wrong.

I think it helps to instead think of your body as a demanding piece of machinery that you have to work with in order to live your life to the fullest. Whether or not you like the way your body looks in jeans is irrelevant to this chapter. It doesn't matter if you are a size zero; you're still at risk of a heart attack later in life if you don't work out and watch your diet. You can love your curves, but it doesn't mean sleep deprivation isn't going to weaken your immune system or tempt you into snooze-ville while you're behind the wheel of a car.

Think of your body as a vessel, not as an avenue to self-confidence. Taking care of your health will lead to self-confidence, sure, but not for the shallow reasons a lot of magazines would have you believe. You'll feel more confident because you'll have more energy, and exercise releases feel-good endorphins. You'll also feel more confident because taking care of your body is a way of showing yourself you are worth loving. This confidence will translate into pursuing the opportunities you deserve in your career and demanding the respect you deserve in relationships. Caring for yourself is pivotal to getting it together and achieving the successes you desire. The time you spend making healthy choices is time you spend on you. It's like you are your own lover—drawing yourself an Epsom salt bath, taking yourself on long runs on the beach, or curling up with yourself for a long night of sleep. Don't learn to love your body; learn to show love to yourself.

TWENTYSOMETHING FACT(ish)

It is just now hitting 87 percent of twentysomethings that their parents let them eat Lucky Charms—literally just a pile of marshmallows—for breakfast every morning. I mean, what?

REAL LIFE SURVIVAL STORY
Running Away

People say it's normal for twentysomethings to become unhealthy when they're in relationships. One reason for this is that, once you have someone to lie on a couch and eat pizza with every Saturday, what exactly motivates you to stay fit? Come on, happy couples! This is really just lazy!

But another, more insidious reason that people in relationships sometimes get out of shape is because they are unhappy. Maybe they are mad at themselves for sticking with a person who makes them unhappy, and, deep down, they've decided they don't love themselves enough to give the simple gift of good health.

My friend Amanda found herself out of shape for the latter reason. Depressed, she came home from work every day, ate comforting carbs, and watched TV. Then one day, out of solidarity for a coworker, she signed up for a 5K. It felt good to have a reason to work out, and the more she did it, the more confidence she had. The more she took care of herself, the more she realized she deserved to be cared for and feel happy. She realized that there really was life that existed outside of her cycle of sadness. When Amanda finally had the courage to end her relationship, she comforted herself not by drinking or binge eating, but by running. Years later, in love with a new boyfriend, she realized they both loved hiking, playing tennis, and being active together. It was a long way from the nights she had spent silently in front of the TV.

When all else feels hopeless and you're not sure what exactly is making you so damn sad, start by working on yourself. Show yourself love by caring for your physical well-being. Finding a path that's more suited to your happiness and fulfillment gets much easier from there.

"DOCTOR FEEL GOOD" ABOUT YOURSELF

Ready to start loving who you are? First, take yourself out on a date . . . to the doctor's office. Physical well-being is not all about body image; it's about body maintenance. Letting doctor visits slide to the bottom of your list of priorities is a dangerous rut to get into because it allows issues to go undetected and snowball, making them more expensive and disruptive to fix down the road. Lucky for twentysomethings, there is a good chance your body doesn't demand high medical bills or inpatient care too often. Going to the doctor when you're young, for the most part, is all about vigilant preventative care.

By preventative care, I don't mean looking both ways before you cross the street. I mean, you have to get regular checkups even if it feels like your career will come crashing down if you leave work for an hour. Your dentist loves teeth enough that she studied and stared at pictures of them for years, so let her help you prevent cavities. That's all she wants. Also, don't skip physical therapy after an injury or you are doomed to repeat it. These things and more fall under preventative care.

But you knew all that. The trick is getting all this paid for.

Paying for Your Doctor Appointments

Yes, doctor appointments cost money; money that you may not feel you have. But while you feel financially broke now, if you cheap out on preventative care, you'll feel physically broke sometime in the near future. Inevitably, you will get sick or break a bone, and lacking insurance not only decreases your feasible care options, but it can also result in unreal medical costs, financial ruin, and certainly government fines. After age 26, when most everyone gets kicked off their parent's health insurance these days, you need to figure out how to get yourself covered. That's just part of the deal when it comes to being a responsible adult. Hopefully, the company you work for offers plans, but you'll still need to pick the one that is right for you. Buy health insurance that is tailored for your needs as a young person and look for a plan that covers preventative care *and* emergencies, and remember that you'll have to buy *separate* dental insurance. But before you can start shopping for a health-care plan, you need to know what you're looking for. Like, literally, what is all this stuff you're looking at.

Here are a few vocab words that are good to know when shopping around.

- **Premium:** The amount you pay for your health-care plan, per month, whether you visit a doctor or not. This is a payment that says, "Hey, you, schedule your regular checkups; otherwise you are not getting your money's worth."
- **Deductible:** The amount of money you'll have to spend on services before your insurance kicks in and starts paying. So if your deductible is $1,000, you'll have to spend $1,000 before your insurance starts to cover your health-care expenses. Once you've hit your deductible, you can just sit back and enjoy all the luxuries your plan has to offer, payment-free!

Well, usually payment-free. There are things they might not cover 100 percent. See "coinsurance." Regular checkups, medication, and emergency room visits usually don't count towards your deductible. Usually, those costs are agreed upon when you sign up for the plan and those are called a . . .

- **Co-payment:** Street name "co-pay." This is the fee you pay upfront for routine checkups, prescriptions, and emergency room visits. Your insurance provider takes it from there. To give you some ballpark figures, checkups are usually around $25 and emergency room visits can cost upwards of $100, depending on your plan. These fees are meant to keep you from visiting the doctor too liberally but may end up making you shy away from visits. Nobody ever said insurance providers weren't cold-hearted snakes. In fact, they usually say that's exactly what they are!

- **Coinsurance:** This is your share of the cost after you've met your deductible. So if you have a $100 procedure after meeting your deductible and your plan requires a 15 percent coinsurance payment, you will owe $15. If you want to put a cool spin on this, you can call yourself a "Coinsurance Provider." Cool title!

- **Out-of-pocket maximum:** The maximum amount you'll have to pay on your own, usually within a calendar year, before you are covered completely. You'll be covered completely after hitting this amount, for real this time. This usually includes co-payments and coinsurance payments. Your premiums or unnecessary medical procedures do not count towards this limit. Under the Affordable Care Act, the out-of-pocket max is around $6,500 for an individual.

That out-of-pocket max may sound like a lot, but that is roughly what I was charged for one CT scan when I was 22 and didn't have insurance. These things add up, fast, and unlike Old Navy, the prices are not the same at every location. Procedures vary from hospital to hospital and insurance is your ticket to keeping prices not only low, but consistent. Luckily for me, after many tears, I was able to provide proof I was very poor and they reduced the charge. I vowed to never be without insurance again. If you cannot prove you are broke, however, medical bills can and will wipe out your savings—and any hope you have of homeownership. Or decent-mattress ownership. So get insurance, and have appendicitis until your heart's content! Don't feel intimidated by doctor visits any longer! The basic rule of thumb for young, healthy people as they shop for insurance is to worry less about the deductible and more about the premium and copayments.

By now you are saying, "Alright, so I can do whatever I want and a doctor will fix me up later? Got it!" Well, no . . . not quite, McSassy! There are a lot of ins and outs to preventative care, like nutrition.

QUARTERLIFE PRO TIP: COVER YOUR MEDICAL EXPENSES, TAX FREE

After picking your plan, calculate about how much you'll be spending, and get a flex spending account so you can pay all your medical expenses, tax free. "Flex whating account?" you ask. More on that when we talk budget in Chapter 7.

YOUR DIET: HOW ARE YOU FUELING YOUR BODY?

In July 2013, Jennifer Aniston told an amazing story to *New York* magazine that made most health-unconscious twentysomethings hate her. Here is the quote:

"I'll never forget when [then fiancé] Justin and I were on a road trip and we were so hungry," Aniston explained. "The only thing around was McDonald's. I think I ordered a Big Mac. Wow, my body did not react well to that! It was like putting gasoline in a purified system. I am always trying to eat organic and natural foods, so that just made my stomach turn and made me feel terrible. And I think what you put in your body, as well as stress, is reflected in the quality of your skin."

Listen, I truly believe that sucking on a McDonald's French fry is the modern day equivalent of sucking the fingertip of a god. That said, Jennifer Aniston is exactly right. Many of the processed foods we've mindlessly accepted into our diets aren't actually doing anything for our bodies. Our bodies did not evolve to digest these foods nor pull nutrients from them. Basically, processed foods are as confusing to your body as drugs are to your brain. Your brain takes in the drug, gets confused, and projects a leprechaun onto your carpet because what the heck were you expecting it to do with those chemicals? Likewise, when you eat too much high-fructose corn syrup, your body just puts that energy into fat cells. What else is it supposed to do? You may build up a tolerance to crap food, quietly turning that food into fat cells without upsetting your stomach like it does if you aren't used to it (like poor, super-rich, movie star Jennifer Aniston), but that doesn't make it healthier. The long-term effects of a poor diet are hard to ignore. It can weaken your immune system, make you feel sluggish, wreck your skin, and may even lead to long-term health issues such as heart disease and diabetes. These are pretty serious consequences, but most people don't begin to think about a nutritious diet until they are well into their twenties. Why not? Blame society.

You see, health knowledge tends to be delivered word of mouth and we twentysomethings have had the misfortune of being raised in the glory days of processed food. When you were growing up, the science of building the most addictive snack was growing exponentially (hello, high-fructose corn syrup!) while the average individual's personal knowledge about health remained stagnant. If you think for one second that twentysomethings *weren't* brought up in a time of especially neglected nutrition, consider the fact that we are the first generation with a shorter life expectancy than our parents.

So how do you begin to undo a quarter century of unhealthy habits? How do you swap out these impure fuels for something healthier that can energize you without making you sluggish in the face of bigger goals, like pitching an idea at work or maybe a romantic mountain hike? Let's start with going back to the basics of nutrition.

The Balance of a Balanced Diet

Think of your body as a paint-by-the-numbers project. Painting the numbered sections with their correct corresponding colors is integral to your finished product. If you were to paint every number with the color brown, that would be a mess. Your teacher may still give you a gold star, but he'll secretly ask your parents if everything is okay at home. Eating overly processed foods that have been stripped of their nutritional value is like painting everything brown. That hurts your big picture. Completely cutting fat or carbs can be just as harmful. You need a well-rounded nutritional pallet. So how do you add some natural "colors" to liven up a "beige" diet of processed foods? What follows are the elements of a balanced diet.

Protein

Key Foods: Chicken, tuna, cottage cheese, eggs, soybeans

Protein molecules are an essential structural element in your body's tissues. Protein is in every cell, building muscle and keeping your hair from falling out. Protein transports nutrients all around your body and strengthens your immune system. When you are exposed to bacteria or viruses, it rushes to the scene of the crime in the form of antibodies in an attempt to keep that shit from spreading. Protein's got your back.

Fat

Key Foods: Walnuts, sunflower seeds, olive oil, salmon, avocados

Fats regulate your body temperature and surround your bones, nerves, and major organs, protecting you from injury and absorbing vital nutrients that would otherwise get flushed out. Fats can also be a backup source of energy. However, not all fats are created equal. Avoid labels with "trans-fat." Anytime a label says, "partially hydrogenated," you can also assume it has trans-fats. This kind of fat contributes to serious health issues in the long run, like heart disease, and it can also disrupt your metabolism and your body's natural ability to burn fat right now, due to its funky, man-made structure. Unsaturated fats, on the other hand, are the good guys. They encompass Omega-6 and Omega-3 fatty acids, which can actually lower your cholesterol.

Carbohydrates

Key Foods: Oats, apples, pasta, rice, peas

Carbs provide energy. You can't get very far without burning carbs. They also release serotonin, a chemical linked to feelings of well-being, in your brain—one reason pasta and chocolate tend to make you feel happy. Carbohydrates not only keep your workouts moving; they contain fiber (see more on fiber later on in this section)—which keeps your bowels moving. Win-win! Plus, carbs help keep you hydrated. Like fats, there are good carbs and bad. Again, it's an issue of how processed the food is. You'll get more carb benefits from whole grains and fruits than you will from overly processed white bread and cookies with refined sugar. While overly processed, carb-heavy foods will do little but provide energy that could turn into fat if unused, eating natural, high-fiber carbs will work naturally with your body to flush out waste.

Fiber

Key Foods: Lentil beans, broccoli, raspberries, oatmeal, whole-wheat pasta

Fiber is an element that gives structure to plants. While our bodies desperately need it, we don't actually digest it. There are two types of fiber. While soluble fibers turn to a gel that helps slow digestion, lowering cholesterol and blood sugar, insoluble fibers hold strong and instead add weight and softness to your stool, making the digestive process much more pleasant. Fiber, as we've covered, is often coupled with carbs, which is why, instead of falling for the ruse that is no-carb dieting, you should instead focus on good carbs that are not processed and keep their fiber grams intact.

Water

Key Foods: Whiskey—just kidding! Water.

Water keeps things clean. It moves waste through your body and keeps your joints moving smoothly. If you aren't drinking water, you might as well think of your body as full of cobwebs. Yeast infections, zits, fever—these are your body's cobwebs. So drink water!

So now that you've got the elements of nutrition down, how much of them should you eat daily? What percentage of protein do you need vs. fat? Balancing these in your diet may take a bit of getting used to after spending your early twenties eating nachos by bar light. There is a mathematical way to figure out the ratio precisely, but why waste your time? The best way to learn is to learn as you go by keeping track of what you eat via an app, like Myfitnesspal, or a website like the MyPlate feature at *www.livestrong.com/myplate*. Don't go into nutrition-tracking thinking of it as a diet; think of it as assessing where you are at now with your nutritional habits. Once you see what your ratio of carbs to fat to protein is and how many calories you are taking in, use the app to start making efforts to even your nutrition intake out to a healthy level. Many sites not only keep track of how many calories you need given your age, height, and desired weight; they also keep track of what percentage of your diet is devoted towards protein, fat, and carbs.

QUARTERLIFE PRO TIP: STOP KEEPING TRACK BEFORE YOU GET OBSESSED

The apps and sites available to help you track your diet can often become addictive. The goal is not to have a meltdown when your friends want to add a side of guacamole to the order after you've accounted only for salsa; the goal is simply to become conscious of whether you are getting the right amount of carbs, fat, and protein. Once you start to feel yourself instinctively knowing what your daily diet should be, stop keeping track and start living. These apps are training wheels; the goal is to ride that two-wheel bike on its own so your friends don't make fun of you next summer!

Health Street Smarts

Once you have the basics of nutrition down and you've down-loaded an app to track your diet, it's time to put your healthy eating plan into action. There are certain actions you can take to make sure your nutrition plan sticks and you're on your way to a healthier and more fulfilling lifestyle. What kinds of habits can you expect to learn on the mean streets of nutrition as you put your healthier diet into action?

Read the Articles—Even if They're Boring

Do not avoid reading articles about nutrition, even if they seem like a total buzz kill. Maybe you feel personally offended when you read an article about how unhealthy Oreos are, but you have to let go of your past and educate yourself! That's what responsible adults do! If blueberries were just ousted by strawberries as the new super-fruit, you, as a human who eats, should know about it. Soaking in this knowledge isn't as intimidating as you think. Go to Prevention .com or Self.com, sign up for their nutrition mailing lists, and let the health tips come to you.

Cut Back on Sugar

If you are going to cut back on anything, focus your efforts on sugar. It doesn't contain any redeeming nutrients, leads to obesity, and can actually accelerate the aging process of your cells. Fat, red meat, and salt have been given a bad name over the years, and those dudes mostly deserve it. Overindulging in any of these things can be hazardous to your health. However, it's much easier to over-indulge in sugar, given that it is hidden within so much of our food.

Look at the labels: pasta sauce, ketchup, yogurt, granola, protein bars—these things are riddled with unnecessarily added sugar. If you find yourself at the grocery store before you've had a chance to do your research, don't panic; shop comparatively. Pick up every brand of pasta sauce to find the one with the least percentage of sugar. Become conscious of what you are putting in your cart. Why take on the added sugar of a protein bar when you can simply grab some nuts instead? Sorry, that came out wrong . . .

Brown Bag It

It's easier to keep track of your diet if you pack your lunch. It'll save money and give you control over your meal—unlike the grill chef who always gives you extra French fries because he has a crush on you. Extra French fries are the last thing I need, Grill Chef! You'll have more control over exactly what you're entering into that nutrition app, giving you a better picture of your overall health. It's this kind of mindfulness that will ultimately lead you to a healthier, less sluggish, and more confident lifestyle.

Avoid Drinking Empty Calories

By and large, any liquid besides water should get the side eye. Most beverages, even the ones claiming to be pure fruit juice, are chock-full of sugar (we talked about this!) or carbonation that will make you feel bloated. Sorry, "Vitamin" Water, you're not fooling anybody anymore. Sticking to water will help to keep your skin clear and your hair fresh, and it will help balance your kidneys and energize your muscles. You see how cutting out other beverages in favor of water will have a plethora of wonderful benefits? That said, you may not want to live in a world where you drink only water at happy hour. So to cut down on sugar after hours, stick to low-calorie drinks like vodka and soda and drink water every other drink to stay hydrated and last longer out with your friends without having to take in ungodly amounts of sugar.

REAL LIFE SURVIVAL STORY
Water It Down

In my early 20s, I moved to New York City and lived with my college friend, John. We were young and usually drunk—intoxicated by the big city but also just regular, alcohol drunk. Our diets left a lot to be desired. John seemed to exist on a diet of chicken nuggets and frozen waffles. His healthiest meals usually involved getting unlimited salad and breadsticks from the Olive Garden and bringing a doggie bag home to me. Obviously, I was all about this setup.

One Friday night, our weekend was off to its usual start—drinking at a karaoke bar. A couple of drinks into the night I noticed that John wasn't drinking anything but water. I was worried about him because, in your early twenties, you tend to think *not* drinking is a sign of depression. John informed me that he was going on a first date the next day—a first date that involved a hot yoga class. Drinking before hot yoga is like drinking before running a marathon. Was John supposed to decline this invite and prioritize drinking? Of course not. He realized that he wanted to start meeting people with interests outside of bars, and he wanted to experience mornings without a hangover. During the next few months, John steadily built a network of workout buddies outside of dating. My eyes were opened to another way of living, and seeing this lifestyle made it impossible to continue down my unhealthy path. John's hot yoga date was Eve holding an apple. John and I were two sad, chicken-nugget-loving Adams, suddenly aware that we were totally and completely nude. We were motivated to take a step out of The Garden of Eden and into the world of getting it together.

Treat Yourself

It helps to assign your favorite treats a special occasion. A lot of people try to keep their diet to about 10 percent treats, but I think that involves too much math. It's easier to just use treats to *treat* yourself. You'll look forward to them twice as much—and they'll be even more delicious with a sweet side of self-satisfaction. Maybe save fast food for road trips and soda for Saturday afternoon matinees. Eat hotdogs at baseballs games and drink margaritas with girlfriends. Then eat chocolate when you really, really want chocolate, and it's all you can think about. Negotiate with yourself as we discussed in Chapter 1, and reward yourself for keeping your diet on track. Exercising this kind of self-control is integral to responsibility, confidence, and becoming successful.

Becoming a healthy eater won't happen overnight. It's a journey, and, one day, if you stick with it, you'll find yourself finally curious enough to look up what the heck "kale" is. (Spoiler alert—it's not a fish. I really thought it'd be a fish.) Now, once you've begun fueling your body properly, it's time to start using that wonderful machine of yours. Remember how carbs give you energy? Well it's time to hit the gym and let those carbs out to play!

WORKING OUT YOUR MACHINE

Human beings evolved to be physical badasses. We ran around the forest, and carried spears that we chiseled out of stone. We were goofy little rascals who wrestled and hunted all the time, keeping our muscles in constant use. Now we're too smart for our body's own good. Why wrestle when you can send angry e-mails? Why carry a spear to catch food when you have a Seamless account? Now that we're a bunch of smarty-pants, we need to actually set aside time to be physically badass. Why should you care whether you are physically badass? Because it'll help prevent physical injury (like pulled back muscles and twisted ankles), which can slow down progress in other areas of your life. Many twentysomethings take their physical strength and energy levels for granted, forgetting that if you do not spend some extra time focusing on your fitness, your energy levels will begin to decline, and your posture will slowly begin to crumble as a life of computers and couches takes its inevitable toll.

If you haven't been making time for exercise, as you get used to working out, you'll find yourself feeling like the whole thing sucks. And that's okay! After all, working out is not supposed to be fun. You are supposed to sweat and your muscles are supposed to shake, and, while this is happening, you should despise anyone who ever suggested you do it. Then, within two minutes of finishing, you'll feel happier than you've felt all day. Have you ever heard someone talk about a "runner's high"? That is a real thing. Exercising releases endorphins that make you feel like you are on cloud nine. Endorphins are chemicals that are released during certain stimuli, everything from sex to stubbing your toe, to block pain receptors or lead to a euphoric feeling. Working out ends with euphoria but begins with misery. There are three different kinds of misery involved in a balanced workout plan: cardiovascular training, weight training, and stretching.

Cardiovascular Training

Cardiovascular training is anything that can get your heart rate up, from running to dancing to jumping rope. Cardio strengthens your heart and lungs, which will then not have to work as hard when you are resting. The goal is to get your heart pounding at its "target heart rate" for 20 minutes, roughly two or three times a week. Your "target heart rate" depends on your age, but, as a twentysomething, yours is most likely between 15 and 25 beats per 10 seconds. So as you work out, just find the pulse in your neck and count the beats for ten seconds. Try to keep those beats up there! You're going to feel so miserable and then so good!

Weight Training

There are so many benefits to weight training, it's a little ridiculous. If you like seeing results, weight training is where the sculpting is. If you want to run longer, it can also increase your endurance. If you are trying to drop weight, your muscles will continue burning energy for hours after lifting. So how do you incorporate this into your routine a couple days a week? You don't necessarily have to venture into the scary, free-weight side of the gym right away; you can start small. Yoga and Pilates are considered strength training since you are working out with your own body weight. Increased weight does not necessarily equal better results; more repetition with lighter weights can be just as effective. Workout videos, which include handweights, are another way to go. Like cardio, you have options and should experiment to find which routine is least miserable for you!

Stretching

Working out can make you feel old if you let it. You'll start to notice consistent back and leg pain, possibly from loosening up your muscles during a workout and then cramping them up behind a desk all day. Stretching after a workout can help stop these symptoms in their tracks because it increases circulation and flexibility and alleviates stress. It's even good to stretch on days you aren't doing a full workout. To learn the best stretches, invest some time and money in a few sessions with a personal trainer. Those guys know where it's at. For what it's worth, stretching is pleasantly *not* miserable.

Stay Motivated

Okay, so now that you know what you *should* be doing, here's how to actually get it done! Yes, I can hear your inner voice saying, "But . . . aren't couches so comfortable? Sometimes they feel like clouds. Like, for real like clouds. So soft! I'll just sit here for 15 more min-ut-es. . . ." STOP. No excuses! Excuses are not part of getting it together amidst the chaos of your quarterlife crisis—excuses will serve only to hide the problems while they snowball. Possible problems include your poor posture caused by your lack of core strength. If you don't want your weak body to stand in the way of your big dreams, get up and get going. Here are some things to consider when you are thinking about skipping exercise.

- **That time you went bowling and your arm was sore the whole next day.** So you picked up a 10ish-pound ball 20–40 times? And you were so sore the next day that it hurt to raise your arm, and you thought it might be some kind of terminal disease causing that pain? Don't you see? It doesn't take all that much for your body to start to feel the burn, so don't be intimidated by the time commitment. Also, next time, don't be the person whose arm is sore after bowling.

- **The music!** Exercise is an excuse to listen to your guilty pleasure music. Ask even the biggest music snob what she listens to while she works out, and she'll either be refreshingly honest or pause awkwardly while trying to think of something to say besides Flo Rida.

- **How awesome it feels to be worn out physically from time to time.** Remember being a kid and being out of breath and how that wasn't a big deal at all? How, as your pulse slowed down, your lungs felt full and refreshed? The fastest way to feel like a kid again (come on, you know you want to!) is to work out super hard.

- **You are sick and tired of being sick and tired.** Getting your blood flowing boosts your immunities. You'll have skin that glows and need fewer sick days. Start using those sick days less for rolling around on the couch in agony and more for playing hooky! I mean, I never do that personally. It's just an idea. . . .

- **They don't call it working out for nothin'.** Working out really does work stuff out. Whenever you're done with a run, you'll feel 1,000 miles away from your cubicle. You'll also feel smug. Sure, that passive-aggressive e-mail you received at work almost made you cry; but now you're in tune with your body's most basic needs, so that means you win, now doesn't it?

- **All you need is one month and you'll be addicted.** You just need to hit that one-month mark. Then you'll notice changes that you won't ever want to let go of. You'll find yourself jonesing for a quick, 20-minute workout the way you used to crave a nap. Well, you'll still crave naps. I put myself down for a nap every Saturday afternoon or else I start to get fussy. But you'll also crave a workout, and there's nothing wrong with that!

Once your eyes are opened to the many benefits of working out—and the idea that going to the gym can actually help you feel happier, avoid injury, and build confidence—choosing to skip a workout in favor of happy hour starts to seem silly. Working out is a cornerstone of preventative care and a skill you'll need for the rest of your life—so start putting in the time now.

PREVENTATIVE CARE SPLURGES EVERY TWENTYSOMETHING HAS EARNED

So sometimes working out and eating healthy can be tough. Do you know what isn't tough? Treating yourself. After all those luxurious days in your early twenties sleeping on an air mattress and wearing underwear until the elastic deteriorated, you'll be glad to know that there are important, minor indulgences that benefit your health—and it's time to splurge! So don't feel guilty when you buy:

- **Shoes:** Shop carefully, make sure you love them, and then spend what you can afford to get shoes that support your arches and look good at work, too. The last thing you want to do after all of your working out is get a stress fracture on your foot from walking around in cheap flats.
- **Daily SPF:** You've been drinking water and eating healthy fats—all great for your skin—so treat yourself to some nice face cream that will also keep the sun from wrinkling your skin.

- **A Neck Pillow and a Lumbar Pillow:** You are a classy, health-conscious adult who is sick of waking up with back and neck pain at the end of every flight. Get that back of yours in line and make all those silly teenagers who are too cool for neck pillows jealous.

TWENTYSOMETHING FACT(ish)

One time, a super-hot guy on a flight hit on me by saying, "Nothing is sexier than a girl who supports her lumbar and browses the in-flight channels, stopping on everything that stars Diane Keaton."

- **A Decent Mattress and an Ergonomic Office Chair:** So much of aging starts with back pain; and, as you approach 30, you'll start to notice there's always one guy at the Oscar party, lying on the hardwood floor to relieve his back pain. Try to avoid being that guy. Splurge on a mattress and chair that will keep your back aligned.
- **A Vegetable Steamer:** The healthiest and easiest way to cook everything from broccoli to spinach is to steam. Steaming doesn't get so hot that nutrients are destroyed like with frying, and, in some cases, it can break down nutrients just enough to help your body absorb them more easily.

- **An Aluminum Water Bottle:** Your water intake will triple during your twenties due to sudden health awareness and the increased length of hangovers, so it makes economical sense to invest in your own bottle. Stick with aluminum because certain plastics break down and become unhealthy to continue drinking from over time.
- **A Great, 30-Minute Workout Video:** The easiest way to squeeze in a quick workout during a particularly busy week is to do a video at home, like Jillian Michaels's "30-Day Shred" or the "YOGAmazing" video podcast series.
- **Sleep:** While you're splurging with cash, don't forget to also splurge on sleep. As we discussed in Chapter 3, sleep is the only way to recharge your body and keep it running at its full potential. Your goal is to maximize your amount of REM sleep cycles per night, a loop which reoccurs about every 90 to 120 minutes throughout the night. During this time, your body repairs itself, and your bone and muscle tissue regenerate. Your immune system also gets a boost. If you make sure to get seven to eight hours of sleep a night, you can squeeze in about four of these sweet, sweet REM cycles. So move up your bedtime and reap the rewards.

Becoming a healthy adult is a balance of educating yourself, discipline, and treating yourself to nice things. It's not a specialty interest—it's a lifestyle that is attainable, so get out there and get it done!

THINGS TO REMEMBER

Developing healthy habits can be an intimidating endeavor. Perhaps, like most twentysomethings, your education on the subject is severely lacking. Or perhaps you just feel hopeless when you think about trying to achieve the "perfect body." But fear not, your body is a clump of cells with a very cut-and-dried set of needs. If Hulk Hogan can (mostly) manage to take care of his, so can you! As you work to get healthy, remember:

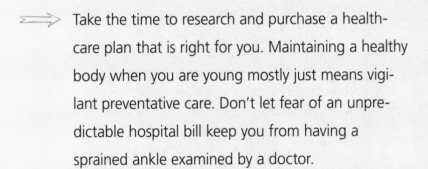 Take the time to research and purchase a health-care plan that is right for you. Maintaining a healthy body when you are young mostly just means vigilant preventative care. Don't let fear of an unpredictable hospital bill keep you from having a sprained ankle examined by a doctor.

Practicing vigilant preventative care also means being thoughtful about what you eat. Fuel your body with the things Mother Nature intended: carbs, protein, good fats, fiber, and water. Avoid processed food and sugars. Keep track of your diet using an app or diet-tracking website.

➡️ There's no way around it; you have to work out. Just know you have a runner's high to look forward to! Make sure to get a proper balance of cardio, weight training, and stretching in your life. Consult a professional if you haven't worked out in a while— they can make sure you are doing it right.

➡️ Go ahead and splurge. Splurge on your health! It may seem nerdy at first, but grab a neck pillow, some comfortable shoes, and a trusty aluminum water bottle, and you can take on the world!

CHAPTER 5

All You Need Is Love . . . *Ugh* Together Now

As you approach thirty and everyone around you becomes attuned to their needs, expectations on the dating scene intensify. Plainly said—"shit gets real!" It can be intimidating to keep up with because everyone's looking for something and someone different. Some people just want to have fun and experiment liberally to see what kinds of people they really click with. Others won't waste time with someone they don't see as a potential life partner. Still others don't know what they're looking for and just need a hug. Yet, among all these interests, a consistency remains—all anybody wants when it comes to dating is to find fulfillment with a partner without losing faith in themselves.

There are ways to make sure you are growing as a person, even while expending energy on getting to know another person intimately. It's important to be sure you are fulfilled and still happy deep down, even when things don't quite go as planned. In this chapter, you'll learn about long-term relationships—a few tricks for staying happy in them and how to know when it's time to break up. Then, because so many twentysomethings end up on first dates with complete strangers due to the rise of online dating and the dwindling reserves of guys you went to college with, you'll get the details on how to date without being a jerk and what taking it slow *really* means. But before any of that, let's peek inside the head of a typical twentysomething and identify some of the mentalities that may be holding your romantic life back.

A TWENTYSOMETHING DATING MENTALITY UPDATE

If you're like most people, you started dating somewhere between the ages of 16 and 20, so it stands to reason that the dating scene in your early twenties is full of a bunch of numskulls who don't know what they are doing. Or at least that's how most dads would explain it to their daughters. There is truth in that. Your first few relationships introduce you to the pure, blinding strength of emotions you never before knew you were capable of. Your early twenties are the only time in your life when the actions of Romeo and Juliet seem reasonable. You can't think clearly, and everything feels threatening, like the first time behind the wheel of a car. You likely formed some bad habits when you were first trying to navigate all this confusion. Well, now it's time to break those habits and start seeing all the signs more clearly. Let's take these bad habits one at a time, starting with how damn lovable you are.

The Curse of Striving to Be Lovable

Many twentysomethings date in order to find someone who loves them when, in reality, you should be trying to find someone whom *you* want to love. You can put some blame for this squarely on the shoulders of the Disney princesses who lead children to believe that romance begins with being plucked from humble obscurity by a prince who knows nothing about you except that you are beautiful and have a laugh like a delicate fairy. A lot of young women go wrong in their early twenties because they are focused more on convincing men that they are special rather than taking the time to figure out whether or not that guy is special enough for them. Men also suffer from this mentality, having been taught to bury their emotions in order to look tough to the outside world. How do you know you're unwittingly falling into this trap? Some sure signs are:

- You haven't eaten all day, but you order a salad for dinner so there's no chance your date thinks you are a gross eater. You forgot what he ordered . . . maybe a burger?
- He barely asks you any questions about yourself, but you hardly notice because you are too busy worrying whether your enthusiastic interest in his trip to the dentist reminds him of his mother enough to feel comfortable with you—but not so much that it's a turn off.
- Any time he mentions another girl, you cringe inside and hope on a scale of one to special, she's his sister.
- When he says something that you don't agree with, you refrain from offering your thoughts on the matter.
- You pretend to like something you hate for his benefit. You don't even tease him about it to playfully air your grievances; instead, you just sink hours of your time into watching amateur wrestling.

Now, I'm not saying that you shouldn't want the person you are dating to think you are special and wonderful. That's an important part of the equation. Plus, everyone wants to be impressive on a date—that's actually pretty fun. Just be sure that when you put your best foot forward, you like the foot your date is putting out there, as well. Otherwise, you are in danger of losing your sense to the whirlwind of trying to impress someone else.

TWENTYSOMETHING FACT(ish)

Fifty-six percent of twentysomethings have pretended to like a band they hate because they thought their partner loved that band, only to find out their partner also hated that band, and they just spent an entire road trip together listening to Nickelback for no reason.

If you aren't careful, you may even find yourself with the kind of person who makes you jump through hoops to win his approval. That's exhausting and slowly chips away at your confidence. So, if you've been dating for months and the guy you're dating has you on the edge of your seat, wondering if he thinks you are special, you should sort of hate him. Really. To hell with him! If you *still* inexplicably want to be with him, then you'll know unequivocally that you've fallen into the Disney Princess trap. You probably—almost definitely—should not be together. So how do you make sure you truly like the person you are dating and protect yourself from losing track of your own needs?

- **Seize the opportunity to disagree with your dates.** If they can't playfully fight, imagine how annoying it will be to have real fights with them. If they can't take a difference of opinion, you probably need a difference of "o-person."

- **Be responsible for your own dates.** It's romantic to be whisked away on preplanned dates, but make yourself responsible for planning a few. If he drags his feet or makes you feel genuinely self-conscious about your choices, don't giggle it off—tell him to take off.
- **Figure out why you're jealous.** We're territorial animals, but before you waste energy feeling jealous at the mention or presence of another woman, ask yourself if this is because you've gotten swept up in the game to be awarded "most lovable person ever" at the end of the night or if you genuinely feel your date is being disrespectful. Is he *trying* to make you feel jealous? If so, that's lame—don't feel jealous; feel offended. But if it's all innocent, move forward with getting to know your date and don't let your competitive side stand in the way of letting him get to know you.

Make the goal of each date to give this guy a chance to genuinely impress you. Learn about him, and let him learn about you so you'll know if a second date is worthwhile. Don't alter your behavior and interests because, ultimately, sparks won't fly if you're holding all of the kindling to yourself.

REAL LIFE SURVIVAL STORY
Realizing You Are Independently Awesome

My friend, Nicole, is a charmer. I call her sunshine because she lights up a room. In her twenties, she dated without a lot of luck, but we couldn't figure out why. She always had a ton of fun with these guys she went out with, but after multiple dates, things always fizzled. Fizzling is natural, but I often wondered how she was able to have such a good time without realizing there was no spark.

Then, after Nicole went on a date with a guy who showed up in his pajama pants and bragged about being unemployed, we figured it out; she was the reason these dates were fun. It was all her. Her sunshine bounced off those goofballs and made them seem as majestic as the moon. Of course, the dates were fun, but that didn't mean she should like these guys, and they didn't merit a sustainable connection. At the end of the day, they weren't a fit for her, but she was too busy being charming to notice. She liked that these guys seemed into her but forgot to make sure she was into them back. Once she was conscious of what was happening, she started to pay more attention to how much effort she put into making a date interesting and fun. This allowed her to spend less time on guys who weren't sparking and more time finding a genuine connection.

Remember that it's okay to be picky; that's how dating works. It's okay to focus less on being likable and more on whether or not you like your date. Being likable? Don't worry about it; you've got that shit down because you do it every day. However, putting a critical eye to the people you date may feel unnatural because it's not something you do regularly. After all, you aren't trying to forge an intimate one-on-one connection with the old lady who lives next door—with most people, you can let things slide. Which leads me to another twentysomething mentality that needs to go: Fear of confrontation.

Fear of Confrontation

Dating is inherently confrontational; you're going to be rejected, and you're going to have to learn how to reject. Many twentysomethings have a tendency to run away from their problems, but when it comes to dating, being spineless amounts to cruelty. Continuing to text with someone you've already decided you don't have feelings for is classic twentysomething behavior. It's not very nice to lead someone on—yet you've decided not to completely cut things off, as if *that* is the thing that would make you "the bad guy." Handling rejection is also difficult. It's hard not to take it personally and feel bruised. No matter how you slice it, dating requires dealing with confrontation, and it is scary.

It's important to the whole process that you evolve and do everything you can to make dating a slightly better experience for all involved. This is a team effort. Mastering the techniques in this section is worth your while because peace in the dating world means learning to deal with confrontation.

Let People Down Easy

If, as you gaze across the dinner table at your potential lover, you realize you aren't really feeling him and don't find it cute when he dabs his lips like he's at a tea party after every bite—congratulations! You've just made a giant leap forward in your journey to true love by making the decision to sort this person out of the pile. Now, it's as simple as reaching deep down within yourself for the strength to take action and let this person know your decision. Piece of cake (with rocks in it). Look, everyone knows letting someone down is hard. But remember, the world is not made up of good people and bad people by nature; it is made up of people who make tough choices and people who crumble when the time comes. Don't crumble; confidently handle this situation, and you'll save this guy some painful guesswork. Find strength in knowing that you are not only allowing this guy to move on; you are also freeing up time and energy to let yourself move on to a relationship that actually fulfills you. So talk to your friends about their dating stories so you know you are not alone, allow them to hold you accountable for following through with the breakup, write out your feelings, do whatever you can to shake out the jitters, and then get to the task at hand: ending things. The more directly you handle dating confrontations, the more clearly you'll be able to understand the feelings that come with dating, which, as we discussed, are basically hieroglyphics when you first start out. Now that you've dug deep for motivation, it's time to end things. "How?" you ask.

- **End the night at a reasonable hour.** While you may need some time to conjure the strength it takes to end the relationship, at least whip up the strength to end the evening. If you stay out for extra drinks, which lead to making out, you'll just confuse the situation.
- **Don't drag out the ending.** Next time you speak to this person, it should be to tell him that you don't think the two of you are a good fit for a relationship. Tell him what you like about him, but be firm about the fact that the chemistry was not right for you. Be kind. When things don't work out after a few weeks, it's not personal—it's dating.
- **When it comes to your approach, show respect.** How do you do it? Every relationship is different, but you should consider the level of intimacy you shared, both emotional and physical, and try to show this person the amount of respect you'd like if the situation were reversed. Acting

really into somebody for a few weeks, and then inexplicably fading him out is the cruel way to go. If it's only been a date or two, a text is probably fine. If you were more intimate than that, suck it up and call or meet for coffee.

- **Dooooooooon't drunkenly booty call this person.** Getting sloshed and calling someone you've dumped is the dating equivalent of eating all of the M&M's out of the trail mix. When dating and sharing trail mix, there is an unspoken agreement to accept the hand you were dealt. That's the way it works. If he wants more from you than you're willing to give, don't be a selfish jerk. Let him go, ya fool!

Discontinuing dates with someone who wasn't right for you takes kindness but also a lot of guts. You deserve a break. So next, just sit back, relax, and accept rejection gracefully.

Accept Rejection Gracefully

If you find yourself blindsided, or even not so blindsided, by someone cutting things off with you—congratulations! You've just made a giant leap forward in your journey to true love. Now you can sort this person out of the pile as well! Yet, although congratulations are in order, it might not feel that way. The need to be loved is strong with twentysomethings. That's normal. Hell, the need to be loved is a staple of humanity. But even though you're hurt, how you handle rejection can go a long way towards your future peace of mind. Lashing out at someone only shuts him up, ultimately depriving you of the honesty you need to achieve closure and move on. Remember that you are trying to build a life, not burn bridges. There is no reset button in life; a year from now you may want to look back on an experience you two shared fondly without having to cringe at your poorly chosen words when things ended—or, let's be real, a year from now you may want to date his friend. So how do you keep from dwelling on this rejection or worse—saying something regrettably petty like, "Whatever, he had a weird forehead"?

- **Get the answers you need.** If you want to ask why he thought it wasn't working, go ahead and ask. It may help you get closure. Just be ready to hear the answer.
- **Keep it together.** You may feel pangs of insecurity, but keep them to yourself for now—this person is not your friend, so do not seek comfort from him. Talk to your real friends about your feelings later.
- **Stay positive.** Do positive thinking exercises when all is said and done. Don't let yourself spiral into the negative feelings of rejection; instead count your blessings and *definitely* call a trusted friend to be like, "But seriously, though, what was up with his weird forehead?"
- **Make a clean break.** Again, don't drunkenly booty call this person, ya masochist!

I don't know about war, but all is not fair in love. You have to play by the rules of common decency. If you simply apply the rules of being a decent human to dating, confrontation is not so bad. If you want to date, you have to be ready for the harsh truths that inevitably come out. And, of course, you want to date. You're a human, right?

Dwelling on the Past

Throughout your twenties, as your dating experience accumulates, you become less likely to keep an open mind. Like Ted

Mosby in *How I Met Your Mother*, you want to see greater meaning in every moment with a former flame even if the most you two shared was Thai food. Your experiences do mean something, yes, but many twentysomethings begin to see mistakes and red flags everywhere instead of focusing on the things that went well. The memory of the pain clouds out the joy. Often because of this, you go into self-preservation mode, and your walls go up. If these walls were all about learning what you want, they'd be a good thing. But you don't want to put up walls based on bitterness. Recognizing a lack of chemistry quickly is a fine use of your newly narrowed twentysomething mind; if a guy doesn't laugh at your jokes, don't waste your time with him. That's an immediate chemistry issue. But there are other ways in which your mind may have narrowed that result in arbitrary slashing and burning. Maybe you are leery of dating another man-child, so you avoid anybody who enjoys comic books. Or maybe he was still in love with his ex, and now you fear all the exes in all the land. Or perhaps, like most girls, you are permanently suspicious of guys who spontaneously play the guitar at parties.

Whatever fear you have, it likely gets you all wound up before your dates. When you live in fear of making a bad decision, you end up treating dates like interviews or arbitrarily cut out people you would have otherwise gotten along with. As hard as it is to let your guard down, dating is not worth your time if you don't let it down just a little. You don't have to bare your soul, but you do have to give yourself permission to do a few things that may alarm your overprotective heart just a little. For example:

- **It's okay to date guys who are similar to one another.** You don't have to bounce from one opposite of your ex to the next. For example, just because it didn't work out with one sensitive guy doesn't mean you should write off all sensitive guys. Maybe you like sensitive guys for a reason, so don't shut that part of yourself down so quickly. Chemistry, and attention to each other's needs, makes for a good relationship, not character traits that encompass a wide variety of people.

- **It's okay not to ask questions about his past relationships for a while.** Digging for someone's baggage is off-putting and gets in the way of learning who he truly is. Focus less on your search for a red flag and more on your date's opinion on movie theater hotdogs—delicious treat or secretly riddled with tetanus? As comforting as it is to sort someone out of your pile based on indisputable facts, chemistry is much harder to find than someone with qualities you can cross off an impersonal checklist. Whether or not he takes criticism well when you tear down his opinions on surviving a zombie apocalypse is more important in the long run than whether or not his ex got the couch in their breakup.

- **It's okay to follow your gut over your head.** Heart, you aren't a part of this. (Ignore your heart *always*. That dude's nuts.) But, as we discussed, your *gut* is the neutral decision-making territory between your head and your heart. Your gut is your intuition—it's been through a lot with you and has been taught to recognize cues before your head has had a chance to process the vibes your date is putting out. Maybe this person is goofy and sensitive or even unemployed, but you still have a good feeling about him. He just feels like a warm presence to you, and you feel safe. Keep an open mind and see what happens.

QUARTERLIFE PRO TIP: YOUR FRIENDS ONLY KNOW WHAT YOU TELL THEM

Until your friends have met the guy you are dating, they know only what you tell them. If your gut likes him, but you're afraid your friends will tear him apart for being unemployed, then don't lead with the thing you are insecure about. Your friends, in an attempt to protect you, will put a magnifying glass on that thing you are already insecure about. It's okay to keep a few things from your friends until your brain has had a chance to catch up to what you think your intuition is telling you. So don't worry too much about what your friends think. . . . Yet.

Dating can be fun if you resist the urge to indulge your fears from the past and instead focus on getting to know the person in front of you. Focusing on who you are with in the moment isn't just about moving away from your past, though. It's also about suspending your dreams of what he'll mean to you in the future until you know him a little better.

Thinking of Your New Man as Your New Best Friend

In your early twenties, it's rare that you find yourself on a date with a complete stranger. You usually meet through friends who can vouch for this guy, and you probably have already met before date one. Maybe you were already friends! That's pretty ideal. However, the older you get, the less likely it is that you are going to fall for somebody who's already been in your life or in your circle of friends. Those guys are either already spoken for or have clearly been segregated to the "friendzone." And yes, you'll likely hear your successful couple friends tell you friendship comes first, but there's a good chance that this advice may not be applicable to the reality of your situation. Sure, people do end up calling their spouse their best friend, but it takes a lot of work to get to that point—and by that time you'll be something more complicated than friends, so why deprive your platonic best friend of his or her title? Friendship is not something you can leap to—and if you try, you stand the risk of destroying the delicate nature of a new relationship. When dating a relative stranger, if you want to gauge his potential as a partner, keep him out of the friendzone by doing the following.

Give Him Some Space

When you're in school, everybody knows each other and, inevitably, when you start dating someone, you are immediately surrounded by friends on many of your "dates." But the older you get, the less of that you can expect, and you have to get used to it. Just as you are working on your independent self, he is working on his, so don't expect to be invited along everywhere he goes—even if he is around other lady friends. As you grow as a couple, those invites will come, but be patient. Sure, you have a right to feel hurt if all of your *friends* go for margaritas and neglect to invite you along, but in a new relationship those rules don't apply. Those invites are on a case-by-case basis. If things go well, you'll be joined at the hip soon enough—so enjoy the independence.

Don't Try to Force Emotional Intimacy

With friendships, the bond usually begins with this amazing, avalanche conversation where you rehash your life story, laugh, maybe even cry—then order another round. Dating is very different. In a romantic relationship, emotional intimacy takes some people longer than others. Guards are up. Maybe you'll both be the kind of people to have the avalanche conversation immediately, but more than likely, that won't happen. Think of your date as a nervous pimply kid, showing up to your door before prom in a bowtie, holding daisies in his shaky hands. He can't talk—he can barely swallow! You, most likely, are also a pimply kid at heart. You are both nervous and very aware of how you are being perceived. If things are going well, you'll be giving each other butterflies for a while, so do not fret if the big, emotional conversations don't happen immediately. That's a rookie mistake. Let the trust and the comfort build at its natural pace, and soon the avalanche will come. But sometimes . . . it just never comes, the butterflies disappear, and you move on from each other. Them's the breaks.

Expect Romance

You can and should expect more from your romantic relationship in terms of pampering than you would expect from a friend. Sure, it'd be weird to expect your best friend to make you dinner after a long day of work, but your new boyfriend should be going out of his way to impress you. Expect your new partner to be thoughtful and mindful of your needs. Buying you a Bud Light while you watch the Knicks game together isn't enough—you aren't "bros." Expect him to check in at the end of the day if he knows you had a big meeting. Expect him to tell you how he feels about you regularly, and, as things progress, expect him to *wait* for you before watching the new episode of whatever nudity-filled HBO show you two crazy kids are both into. You know, modern romance! And you should be thoughtful in return—don't be shy.

QUARTERLIFE PRO TIP:
RESPECT YOUR OVERNIGHT GUEST

Make a habit of cleaning your apartment before a date. Work cleaning into your prep-time, right before you shower. If you bring someone home, no matter how high you are on romance and butterflies, treat that person like a guest. If this person deserves your night moves, then he or she also deserves a friggin' clean towel and a cup of fresh coffee in the morning—in a clean coffee mug! Don't mess around! It is a sad day, indeed, when Motel 8 outshines you.

Like everything as you progress through your twenties, dating takes on more structure as you learn exactly what you're looking for in a partner. Keep up with that self-awareness by making sure you are in tune with your own needs; make sure you are dating people whom you actually like, learn to accept confrontation when things get real, and expect things to progress differently from a regular, friendly relationship. Because, while dating can be difficult for a twentysomething, maintaining a long-term, committed relationship through your tumultuous twenties is even tougher.

THE TWENTYSOMETHING GUIDE TO COMMITMENT

Your twenties are a period of your life that brings a ton of change. You learn a lot about yourself, what your needs are, and what makes you happy. Because you change so much throughout the decade, it's tough to find a long-term relationship with someone who is able to grow along with you. But as tough as it is, there is no good reason for romance to trip you up on your path to finding happiness and leading a successful life—you just have to prioritize the kind of partnership that lets you live.

The most important thing about being a monogamous twenty-something is to keep your eyes wide open. Love is not a fairy tale; there are challenges long after your frog has turned into a prince. There are a few things you need to know in order to be successful in love—how to take it slow, how to accept each other's baggage, but first, and most importantly, how to sustain a long-term relationship. Being in love is one of the most amazing experiences life has to offer, sure, but it's not everything. The real trick is sustaining team spirit together, which serves to prop up the love. While love feels delicate and intangible, team spirit is actionable; and these next steps will help see you through to the end zone (where you can score a touchdown and do the Kid 'N' Play dance together).

Allow Personal Growth

You must make sure both you and your partner are actively finding your own roads to happiness. People don't make *each other* happy; you have to make yourself happy and bring that positivity back to your relationship. For example, if a career opportunity arises that will mean less time with your partner, don't shy away; instead, give the opportunity a shot; and then spend the time you still have together talking about how your future is taking shape. These fresh conversations will help both of you, as a team, begin to see *possibilities* for your future together, instead of obstacles. Don't fear the unknown; embrace it. If your partner is enjoying the company of new people you don't know, don't act on your initial instinct to feel threatened; instead, encourage his new relationships and ask to meet these new friends at some point. Exploring friendships separate from your relationship helps you each to develop as individuals and helps you to build trust as a couple over time. Your partner can go to a bar with his new friends without being tempted by the fruit of another? Good to know! You can too? Even better!

If you notice your partner is in a funk about his life outside of yours, ignoring it could make him feel bitter down the line as he unfairly begins to see your growth as selfish instead of necessary. So encourage your partner to find his own happiness, and make sure he understands how important it is to your relationship that he follows through. You've got his back. You may find yourself thinking, "This is not the same person I fell in love with," and, hopefully, you are absolutely right—and it's for the better.

Learn to Compromise

Talking through disagreements, even when emotions get heated, is important to a relationship because it means you're each trying to find a way to maximize your individual happiness while staying together. The important part is that when those emotions heat up, nobody gets emotionally or physically abusive and the fight ends somewhat quickly in compromise. That compromise should affect things for the better as opposed to bringing things back to business as usual. Remember, a twentysomething relationship is all about that team spirit and navigating the growing pains of this decade together without stunting someone's personal growth. You can't win a three-legged race alone—just ask my ultra-competitive, second grade classmate who dragged my body across the finish line dead last on field day. Following through on the compromise you've each agreed to goes a long way towards trusting your partner and helps each of you to feel like respected, confident adults, as opposed to a little bruised from being dragged for twenty feet.

If you feel that you can't come to a compromise with your partner, there are likely to be some problems in your relationship. If you are not happy with this person, compromise doesn't come. Maybe you just give in because you've stopped caring enough to look out for your own needs, which, I must add, is a terrifyingly slippery slope towards depression-ville. Maybe you stubbornly refuse to accommodate this person because you don't really care about his needs. If either person in the relationship can't give enough to compromise, you need to address it and figure out if you really want to move forward together.

Shake Up Your Routine

As the rest of your life gets a vigorous shake up through your twenties, it might be a bit jarring to come home to a monotonous relationship routine. More than anything else, your Monday night viewing of *Castle* may come to represent a relationship that is not growing with you. You can't bank on the two of you being equally enthusiastic about *Castle*'s comical exploits for the rest of your days—so keep your routine loose, and don't get stuck in this rut; instead, take advantage of the fact that you are both changing. Try some new fall pilots. Try Indian food. Travel. Make sure you are in tune with each other's interests as they evolve—never let that conversation stagnate.

Mind Your Manners

Don't take each other for granted. Thank your partner when he washes the dishes—every time he washes the dishes. Let him know you appreciate him. When someone you aren't romantic with sends you a gift, you send a thank you note, so why lower the bar for your partner? Write your man a sincere note letting him know how appreciative you were the night before, when he respected your wishes not to gun down any *Grand Theft Auto* videogame hookers in your presence. Acknowledge when your boyfriend slows down and recognizes something you are having anxiety about and squashes it for you. Return the favor, and alleviate his worries whenever you can.

This is really just about respecting your partner's feelings and letting him know you're still in love. Think about it. It's hard to know you are doing something right if nobody tells you, and it's even harder to want to keep doing that thing right if nobody seems to notice your efforts. If you're truly in it for the long haul, don't get into a twentysomething bad-manners rut; start good habits now. Be a team player and make respect a priority. It'll help you each feel more confident going out into the world and tackling those other twentysomething woes that are standing in your way. You don't get to slack off just because you're in love—so mind your manners, lovebirds!

Take It Slow

Parents, media and abstinence-only education may have led you into your twenties believing that "taking it slow" meant withholding sex for a certain number of dates. Advice to "take it slow" is often synonymous with conventional fuddy-duddies who don't know how to embrace the moment and let love rule. But, in reality, "taking it slow" is smart advice with bad marketing.

People often try to impose hard milestones on the pace of a relationship. Milestones like sex after three dates, talk about where this is headed after a month, "I love you" after six months, "Facebook-official" after eight, etc. They do this because they are uncomfortable with the lack of science behind falling in love. The thing is, everybody is different. The rate at which you reach these milestones is specific to *you*. They may not even come to you in a conventional order. What "taking it slow" really means is taking it at your own pace. For example, if you trust somebody enough to start leaving a toothbrush at his place but still shy away from talking about your parent's divorce or being bullied in sixth grade, cut yourself some slack. It's important that you get there, but follow your intuition, not the "rules" of intimacy. If you force yourself to become intimate, emotionally or physically, out of pressure to remain on a timeline, you'll find yourself fighting with your new boo because you feel exposed and insecure before your new partner knows you well enough to calm your fears.

Follow Your Intuition

The nice thing about relationships as you get older is that your intuition is stronger. For example, maybe you've learned that you are the type of person who gets paranoid if you have sex before you know your relationship is monogamous. That is okay! Don't put all your eggs in one relationship basket just because you're insecure about making your partner wait. Go ahead and make him wait while you date around for a while. Likewise, don't feel like you are "easy" just because you are able to get down before you are able to bare your soul. Just be sure to do a gut check at all stages of your relationship to make sure you are fulfilled and aren't compromising your needs to make someone else happy. You'll know you are moving at the right pace if things seem fairly simple and emotional manipulations seem crazy and unnecessary.

QUARTERLIFE PRO TIP: MANIPULATING VS. EXPRESSING

When you are hurt or upset, it can be hard to tell if you are manipulating the person you are dating or if you are genuinely expressing the way you feel. The difference is whether or not you've been upfront. If you are giving the cold shoulder to elicit a reaction without at least saying, "I just need to be alone right now," that's manipulative. If you are upset, clearly indicate it; even if you aren't ready to lay out why.

Saying I Love You

When it comes to finally saying, "I love you," there is no science to the timeline. You just have to make sure you are doing it for the right reason—you *do* love him. The biggest mistake people make is saying, "I love you" instead of, "We're on the same page, right?" "This is going well?" "We're bonkers for each other?" If all you want is reassurance, be aware that that is your need.

If you really do love somebody, you'll say it because you cannot *not* say it. If this person does not love you back, you won't feel like you've made things weird by dropping the "L" bomb—you'll feel like you've done right by your own happiness, and then you'll continue your search for someone who will love you back. If he does say it back? Awesome! Don't pick apart the fact that you were the one that said it first. He *would* have said it first, but he wasn't *quite* as confident in his intuition as you are. Don't second-guess yourself; if you are honest and true to the relationship pace you want, everything will work out the way it should.

Ah. "Everything will work out" is always so comforting to hear. It's like a pat on the head and a juice box. You're young and in love and the world is your oyster! Except, whoops, you can stop wondering about those exes. . . .

Accept the Ghosts of Relationships Past

So you have now found the right pace for yourself, and all is well in your dating world—except for the fact that it's haunted by the poltergeists of relationships past. They're all over Facebook, Instagram, your favorite bars. . . . The older you get without settling down, the more exes you will accumulate. Feeling traumatized by your own dating past can lead to a lot of the harmful mentalities we've already discussed—fear of not being lovable, fear of dating the same kind of guy over again, fear of not being "best friends" fast enough. But it's not just your old flames haunting this beautiful relationship mansion you've built; it's your dude's.

What's important is that you don't indulge the fears these ghosts elicit without talking it through reasonably with your partner first. It's normal to have these fears, and you aren't crazy to want to talk about them. Establishing your right to discuss your feelings and get respect in return is essential to fulfillment and establishing calm in your life. After all, you've got more important things to worry about—like purchasing hand weights so you can stop working out with soup cans. You don't have time to beat yourself up; that shit takes all day, so cut to the chase and directly address the fears your partner's past brings up. Fears such as . . .

The Fear That He'll Treat You Like He Treated His Ex

If your new lover is a sociopath, you should probably run because he ain't changing. But the most *common* reason relationships don't work out is simply because the love wasn't there. There is rarely a clear-cut bad guy—so if your partner tells you that his ex felt he was emotionally unavailable, don't cast him as the villain in your head. Instead, use this information to your advantage. At times when he seems hesitant to share with you, don't get mad; instead, share with him—try to get a dialogue going if it's important to you. You are now with this person because he wants to be with you, so help him get things right this time. People don't just grow within the confines of each relationship; they grow slowly over time from one relationship to the next. You don't necessarily need to lose sleep worrying that your partner hasn't learned from his mistakes. But, if he doesn't want to do better this time, it could be a sign the love is not there.

The Fear That He Is Still Into His Ex

We're animals and we are territorial, so the fear that your guy is still interested in his ex is a natural fear to have. You just can't give in to it unless you have cause. Imagine how you would feel if someone you were really into kept accusing you of still loving your ex—not just any of your exes, but your ex who was in a Creed cover band, always talked with his mouth full, and, ugh, you can't believe you ever dated that guy! That accusation would be frustrating—so don't be frustrating to others. Keep your fears in check by focusing on how your relationship is currently progressing—are you happy? If so, great! Keep doing the things that are working—an ex is no match for a happy relationship. If you still have a small bit of insecurity, just say so plainly—not angrily—to give your boyfriend a chance to sing your praises. That said, if your boyfriend gives you cause for concern, ask him to talk to you about what's going on with this ex. Silently letting your imagination run wild is counterproductive to building a bond.

The Fear That You Are a Monster for Not Being Friends with Your Exes

Whether or not you can be friends with an ex is a hot topic for debate. Maybe you feel that you can't be friends with your ex because, as hard as you try, there will always be a very, very small part of you that is rooting against everyone he dates after you. Let your ego have this one. You aren't a monster! But just because you've made a choice to ditch exes, doesn't mean your current partner should have to draw the same hard line. After all, it *is* possible to be friendly with an ex without wanting to hop into bed with her all over again. Just make sure you feel respected by your boyfriend's level of friendliness with his ex. For example: If they are regularly hanging out alone, oh hell no. Let him know how you feel about this and that you won't be written off as insecure. Tell him there is a tangible boundary that you need to see drawn, and your faith in him depends on it.

The Bottom Line

Maintaining a monogamous, long-term relationship for any length of time in your twenties is no small feat. It requires taking things at your own pace, paying attention to detail, and acknowledging that you're each going to make giant leaps forward as an individual during this decade. Focus on finding your own happiness and encouraging whomever you are with to find his. Being a part of a team like that is rare and impressive. Nothing is more beautiful than a deep connection that has been emboldened by time and challenges. But . . . sometimes it's just not working, and you have to admit that to yourself.

HOW TO KNOW WHEN IT'S TIME TO BREAK UP ALREADY

Many twentysomethings commit to relationships that they haven't thought through because they are young and plan on being young forever. Maybe they even do the whole cohabitation thing because like, eh, whatever, right? Parents just don't understand! But as we've established, you change a lot in your twenties. Priorities change. The commitment starts to feel too deep. The stakes have gotten too high. You don't even know who you are anymore! Is anyone else hot, or is it just you??

Many of your mid-twenties comrades have been silently torturing themselves about the state of their own relationships. You aren't alone, and, odds are, you are all making this too complicated. If deep in your gut, you are not happy, then you should not be with your partner. Simple as that. Entertaining other options while remaining with him is selfish. The problem is, when you are in a long-term relationship that has been set to autopilot as long as you've been an adult, something as simple as knowing whether or not you are happy inside is surprisingly difficult. Google searches don't look into your soul (yet). But identifying areas of your life you are no longer happy with is an important part of becoming a successful and fulfilled adult. How else will you know where to focus your quarterlife survival efforts? There are a few signs you can look out for that may signify that you are no longer happy with your boyfriend and need to move on.

- Do you say things that if you heard a friend say, you'd call her out for rationalizing? "I'm not sure if he's right for me, but at this point I'm too old to be single," "I don't know if it's possible for me to really be in love, anyway," "I love him like a brother!" Well then, try making this your new mantra—"I deserve true inner peace and happiness."

- Do love songs make you uncomfortable? Does the everlasting love concept behind Al Green's "Let's Stay Together" feel as elusive as the Easter Bunny? Songs about love should connect you to humanity, not embitter you. You're way too young to be bitter. Take a long hard look at your relationship if you are.

- Do you fantasize about your partner cheating on you? "Wait, you cheated on me? Ugh. I guess I'm single now!" Break up already!

- Do you often think to yourself, "but it's not him, it's me!" Let's say this is true—that your partner is perfect. He is Ryan Gosling, and he loves braiding your hair and making ice cream sundaes for you. Still, you aren't happy and feel as though you are living a lie. Let your partner move on. He deserves to be with someone whom he makes happy and who loves rocking a braid. And, you deserve to focus on your own happiness.

Listen. The truth is, yes, everyone is flawed. There are things you can accept about your partner and things you can't. Relationships have rough patches, too. People love to tell colorful stories and nitpick little relationship details, but the only reason relationships end is because somebody just wasn't happy the majority of the time. The scale tips too far. Recognizing whether or not you are happy, deep in your gut, is a muscle you have to exercise. You have to work it out, or it gets flabby. So start exercising that muscle. Figure out where your doubts are coming from and if you are happy. If you are not, there is no decision to be made, just action to take. You have to break up already.

No matter how scary it seems, you'll find a way. Be succinct and honest. Don't beat yourself up. You haven't failed. You've just reached a point in your life where you're starting to know what you want. Ending this painful and confusing segment will open you up to opportunities you didn't even know existed. When you choose happiness, the other side *is* greener. And made of candy! That impossible green color comes from the fact that it's factory processed sugar candy! Yay! Trust me, breakups are tough, but you're doing the right thing for yourself and for your future.

THINGS TO REMEMBER

Dating is work because becoming aware of your own needs while simultaneously building your intuition regarding a new, intimate partner is a juggling act. But if a stupid clown can juggle fire, you can juggle your own happiness with someone else's. Remember:

 Everything changes throughout your twenties, including the way people approach dating, so you need to be ready to adjust your mentality. Make sure to focus not just on being likable but also on whether or not you like the person you are on a date with. Do not fear confrontation. And don't expect a relationship to progress in the same way a friendship does.

 Don't let your fear of making the same mistake twice turn into a fear of dating. You have a type you are attracted to. Failing once doesn't mean the entirety of men who seem like your type are wrong for you. You don't always have to date your ex's opposite. Instead, focus on dating someone who satisfies your intuition.

Making a long-term relationship last through your twenties is tough because of all of the changes you're each experiencing individually. Focus on growing together by encouraging your partner to find his passion and keeping your routine loose enough that it allows for you both to shake things up.

 Sometimes, even after years of effort, relationships just plain do not work out. You need to listen to your intuition and hold steady in the knowledge that you are deserving of true fulfillment.

CHAPTER 6

Keeping Some Friendships Afloat, Letting Some Sink, and Other Puns

Whether or not you are in a monogamous romantic relationship, you're still dating around. Always. Friendships require effort, too. Don't be afraid to buy your BFF flowers! But, as with any relationship, friendships have hurdles . . . especially for twentysomethings.

Nurturing friendships is important because your friends are the people in the trenches with you. The people who know you well, have your best interests at heart, and therefore can help find the most successful path for you through any challenge life throws your way, including career change-ups, relationship stress, and even dance work-out classes that you're too intimidated to try alone. I mean, have you heard of Zumba-Yoga-Booty-Ballet and did that name make your head explode? Throughout this chapter, you'll learn how to escape from the rut of taking friendship for granted. Whether you're dealing with competitive friends, trying to control your social media consumption to help maintain healthy friendships, or struggling to hold on to a friend in the wake of a romantic relationship—yours *or* your BFFs—the first step is identifying who is actually worth your time. After all, the trick to fulfilling friendships is focusing the bulk of your attention on a few people whom you truly connect with.

FOCUSING ON QUALITY FRIENDS OVER QUANTITY

In your twenties, a lot of new people enter your life, and, because kicking off your adult life can feel lonely, you most likely allow the majority of those new people right in without much vetting. Be careful! You have to be critical of the people you become close with, not necessarily because people are bad, but because you just won't click with everyone, as nice as they may be. The more time you spend with someone with whom you don't feel comfortable, the more alienated and alone you will feel in general, which doesn't help on your path towards finding success and fulfillment. How do you know if you're just going through the motions? There are a few general ways to identify when a friendship is not working out.

- **She never lets you off the hook.** You're usually reliable, but when you missed a night out because you just plain forgot your friend was organizing one, she curtly says, "It's fine," but refuses to give you the satisfaction of a reassuring smile.
- **You feel sad and misunderstood at the end of every hang out.** Your friend always seems unimpressed with what you have to say, even after that time you got lost in the Amazon rainforest for three weeks and survived with only the clothes on your back and a ballpoint pen.
- **You can't hang out without alcohol.** Even after you've both had an amazing day and all signs point to enthusiastic and happy dinner conversation, things between you always sort of feel awkward—like somebody farted—unless you can get good and drunk.
- **She doesn't like your other friends.** She doesn't even seem amused when one of your friends re-imagines the classic, "That's what she said," joke using the voice of Borat. (That's what she tells me!)
- **She tries to pass insults off as jokes.** After you got up the nerve to tell her it hurts your feelings when she calls you a pushover, she apologized and started calling you a pussy instead.
- **You kind of feel like a bad person after you hang out with her.** Your morals just don't seem to match up, but you keep your mouth shut because you can't think of anything nice to

say after she told you she enjoys fat shaming her 14-year-old niece. And the fact that you kept your mouth shut makes you feel complicit. "Dun Dun!" (In the style of *Law & Order*.)

- **You kind of feel like a bad person after you hang out with her . . . this time because she seems horrified by everything you do.** She can't believe the number of people you've made out with is in the double digits! "Dun Dun!" (In the style of *Law & Order: Criminal Intent*.)
- **You feel like you are doing all the work.** You are the one who is always making plans. You are the one who is always driving the conversation. It's exhausting!

If this is somebody you truly care about, there is a chance you can talk through most of these things, and it's possible that if you let this person remain in your friend circle without being her bestie, you'll both eventually grow into having more in common. But for now, there is a good chance you need to turn down the heat on this relationship. The good thing is that you can do this with friendships because, friends tend to drive in and out of your life freely.

TWENTYSOMETHING FACT(ish)

Susan B. Anthony and Elizabeth Cady Stanton defined the women's movement, but didn't realize they were made to be besties until they ditched the suffrage gang for a night and got some Froyo, just the two of them.

How to Date Your Friends

Once you've found people with whom you click, don't be afraid to let them know it! The biggest mistake a twentysomething can make in the midst of all the changes this decade brings is to take her friends for granted. Putting thought into how you treat your friends isn't manipulative or calculated; it's nice. Waiting for people to call you because you're shy and afraid they'll think you're needy isn't polite; it's selfish. When you have conversations with someone you care about, your genuine good nature shows through with very little effort, but in between those conversations, you have to keep the friendship romance alive. Since, in your late twenties, you aren't going to conveniently run into your friends regularly in your daily life anymore, you have to put some thought into making the love last. Take these steps to make sure your favorite people know they aren't taken for granted and your happy adult life involves them at your side.

Don't Be Afraid to Branch Out

If you really dig someone, make an effort to branch outside of the group every now and then to hang out one-on-one so you can become, or stay, close friends. It's a little scary at first to remove the comfort of a group setting in which every silence is filled with irreverence, but to get close with someone you really like, you have to put on a brave face and ask your friend to dinner. Don't let the moment pass when you realize you both want to see the same movie—make plans. You need to give true friends your undivided attention from time to time in order for the relationship to grow. If you let your guard down and go out on that limb—that limb where it's just the two of you—you'll be rewarded with a real, lasting connection.

Make Your Friend Feel Special

Make sure your friend knows she is special to you. Quick "This made me think of you" texts and e-mails are sweet—don't be shy! You don't have to lavish your friends with expensive gifts to keep them around; you just have to reach out.

In addition, you're going to have to occasionally do things you don't like to do. If it's your friend's birthday and she wants to sing karaoke, even though you personally hate karaoke, you have to suck it up and sing—and you should encourage everyone else to do the same. If your friend does poetry readings, you have to show up to watch every now and then, even if you are busy, the shows are held in a moldy basement, and poetry readings makes you nervous due to their raw, emotional nature. Friendships are about mutual support, and your friend will reciprocate in kind. You can't grow into a well-rounded person if all of your interactions are on your terms—you have to get out there and give love to get it.

Love Your Friends for Who They Are

The more time you spend understanding your friend's happiness and interests, the more the friendship will expand your worldview and give you each the confidence you need to grow. Recognize your friend's feelings as valid, on issues big and small. If your friend likes someone whom you hate, insisting she is crazy unless she rolls over and agrees with you is bad form. Love your friends for who they are. If you want to love a clone of yourself, science might get you there in a few decades, but even then it hopefully won't be socially acceptable to stroll around town with your goddamn clone.

Love Your Friends Enough to Acknowledge When They Are Being Weird

Another side of loving your friend is being there when the going gets rough, so don't be afraid to speak up when you think your friend needs some tough love. Don't confuse unconditional love with unconditional approval. Especially if your friend is being self-destructive or putting you in unfair situations, you must love her enough to call her out, even if she's temporarily offended. You are allowed to have feelings—you're in this friendship, too! If you remain silent, you and your friend will inevitably drift apart. Keeping someone you care about in your life through the hard times also means not taking everything your friend does personally. If she is being sort of a bummer, get to the bottom of it instead of writing her off as a jerk. Listen to what's bumming her out, and try to cheer her up. Jokes or sass work best. Pizza is a close third.

REAL LIFE SURVIVAL STORY
Getting Over Myself

I grew up in a time before social media, texting, or even e-mail. It was a time known as the 1990s. When the technology finally reached my fingertips, I was slow to make it a part of my daily life. I'd have amazing conversations and make connections with people at parties and then just sort of hope to run into them at the next party, never exchanging info or getting the digits. I suppose it was a lack of confidence that held back my technical advancement. I was always telling myself that less of me was more and, therefore, texting and e-mailing added too much of me to the lives of others. I hid behind work to keep my life busy, but though my time was full, my heart longed for stronger friendships. I had friends around me, but thought I was as close with them as they wanted me to be and would often think better of texting them when they were on my mind.

The day I got my first promotion, I told a few of these friends, and the outpouring of excitement and support was humbling. One of my friends insisted on immediately grabbing drinks that night. I felt silly—why had I never gone out of my way to make her feel this special? Because I was caught up in my own head! It occurred to me that my behavior, which I'd always categorized as insecure, was actually selfish. The tools to communicate were right at my fingertips, and I'd sat on my hands. You have to put yourself out there so other people feel better about putting themselves out there. All it takes to solidify a friendship is tearing down a tiny wall and pouring out the feelings you already have.

Stepping Outside the Bar Scene

Having better friendships isn't just about focusing on quality people over quantity; it's sometimes about sharing quality experiences, instead of always going to the bar. Bars get old. Sure, when you first turn 21, they are exciting. After years of being shut down by cranky adults, you can finally join them, and it is glorious. Adults are mostly annoyed by your presence, sure, but you have a license to drink, gosh darn it. So you are going to drink too much and get sick in the bathroom while your new adult friends patiently wait in line. It is your right.

However, after a few years, the triumph of being allowed to drink a beverage wears off. It's no longer funny to wake up and find a forgotten receipt for a round of ten whiskey shots in your pocket—it's more like, "dammit, drunky, I got bills to pay!" Sometimes bars provide magical nights full of endless laughter, but a lot of times they really aren't worth the cash or the caloric intake. As health becomes a more central part of your life (remember what we talked about in Chapter 4?), the way you choose to socialize may become an issue. As much as you love your friends, bars can be exhausting because your time spent hung-over increases with age. Odds are your friends are doing some rut busting of their own and will welcome this new era of bonding. It may feel like there aren't a ton of options, but let's take a moment to think about all the ways you can socialize outside of drinking your life away at a bar. No offense, classic-sitcom *Cheers*.

- **Have a girl's night.** The good old-fashioned girl's night is one of life's simplest pleasures. You just pick someone's place, bring a dish, and start talking. It's super fun to actually be able to hear each other talk without pounding music. Plus, I don't know why, but someone always reveals a secret in this setting. Hey, now that's fun, right?
- **Sports!** Tennis, wiffle ball, bowling—it's fun to be active, and it's also a great way to get to know people. Offering to buy someone a drink can be a dead end. Announcing you'll own them at bocce ball opens the door to a genuine dialogue—trash talk.
- **Take classes.** Not a nerd class (unless that's your thing); the kind where you meet new people and feel great after. My

friend and I used to frequent a cheap yoga class, and, long story short, I haven't laughed that hard about farting since I was ten.

- **Pretend to be a tourist.** Sometimes it's fun to head to the most famous part of your city and live it up, novice style. Vacations can be expensive so do the next best thing—pretend to be on vacation!
- **Go to an event.** Whether you go to see a cheeseball in concert, like Pitbull, or hit up your local library's "How to Become a Mystery Writer" panel, it will be a good bonding experience with your friend. The experience may be enriching—or it may just be a good laugh. Who knows? That's the fun of it.

The bottom line is that it's important to identify the people you feel a true bond with, and treat them well—don't be shy! Ask them on dates! Shake up your activities! Let the people in your life know how much they mean to you because happiness and fulfillment comes from fulfilling others. That said, as much as you fulfill each other, friendships are not without their hurdles. Distance makes the heart grow fonder, sure, but so do minor squabbles. . . .

HOPPING FRIENDSHIP HURDLES

Part of taking friends for granted is neglecting to put the time in when there is a wrong you need to right. If you want to build a better life and find fulfillment, you have to find the strength to face situations that make you nervous. Sometimes, being friends is about as easy as it is for Kermit the Frog to be green—which is to say it's not that easy. And Miss Piggy is always on your back. As frustrating as it is when you have differences with a friend, odds are those hard times will eventually bring you closer together. So let's run through some of these hardships and discuss tactics to make them "easy-ships." Less-hardships? You get it.

Reasons and Seasons

Whether they are coworkers, lovers, or friends, people tend to be in your life for reasons and seasons. In your early twenties, that may be a difficult concept to wrap your head around. You haven't had that many varieties of "reasons and seasons," and, as we've discussed, most of your life up until now has had a built-in reset button every few years. But as you get older, you'll start to notice the intensity of certain friendships decline and some friendships even disappear completely, which can be painful. This is normal! Everyone is changing. You may find some relationships heat up because you've become your friend's source of strength while she goes through a breakup; then you lose track of her for a bit as she emotionally levels and branches out. Maybe you're both new to a city and cling to each other for that reason; then, as you make new friends, your bond slowly comes apart. Or maybe, and this one is painful, she was friends with the person you were dating and didn't pick your side in the split.

The fastest way to healing is accepting that this is painfully and ridiculously . . . normal. You can continue to reach out for a while, if you want, but if she isn't really committing to plans, don't take it too personally. Neither one of you is necessarily a bad person; you are just puppets of time, beholden to the ebb and flow of your daily lives. "Puppets of Time" sounds like a folk song from the '70s. Those folk artists were always so wise. Do your thing, let your friend do her thing, and accept that you don't need to be in regular contact to still care about each other. Keep this person in your life with the occasional "Remember when . . . " text or yearly holiday card. As each of you evolve over time, there is a good chance you'll one day find yourselves on the same page again and be glad you're still on good terms. When things are good and clicking, though, it's important to be a good friend. You're a puppet of time, but that doesn't mean you can't be a nice, giving puppet.

QUARTERLIFE PRO TIP: #TBT

Want to give a nod to an old friend who's faded a bit from your life? Throw up a #TBT (throw back Thursday) photo of the time someone snapped an awkward photo of the two of you eating Doritos in your dorm room freshman year. Look at those baby faces!

Friends in Relationships

Just as it's hard to let go of a friend who's on a different page, the hardest part about having a friend fall in love is letting her go a little bit. After all, it's only natural for a romantic relationship to storm in and dominate your friend's time and, if all goes well, her heart. There are a lot of popular sayings that may indicate you have a right to be openly angry about this, such as: "sisters before misters," "bros before hos," and "girls before Earls." (I may have made that last one up.) The thing is, you really can't be angry. If you've been ditched a few times and this becomes a trend, you can go ahead and call your friend out for ignoring you. That's fair. But if your friend is seeing you less to accommodate a new boo, you have to accept and support. *Accept* that this won't last forever because, at some point, this new flame won't require as much maintenance and will burn steady. Your friend's life is just experiencing growing pains. *Support* that your friend is trying to find fulfillment, and you want to see her happy. "Operation Accept and Support" has only three ground rules:

1. **Don't trash talk your friend simply because she is in a relationship.** Yes, you love her and you miss seeing her as often as you used to, but don't express your hurt in the form of anger. Think of your friend's new focus on her relationship as a vacation. If your friend went on vacation, would you go around telling everyone that she's changed, and now she seems to think that cocktails adorned with tiny umbrellas are the center of the universe? Or would you patiently water her plants, and allow her to return to a happy, nonjudgmental circle of friends?

2. **Insist on meeting this new person in her life.** You don't need to administer an "Are You Good Enough for My Friend" test, but you do need to show an interest in this new, big thing your friend has going on. Be warm and insistent about meeting her new boo, even if you'd rather just hang out with your friend one-on-one. Odds are your friend is super excited for the two of you to meet, and she wants the go-ahead to invite him along on your dinner plans. It's important!

3. **Don't give your friend a guilt trip because you miss her.** A critical aspect of loving someone, including a friend, is genuinely rooting for someone else's happiness. You *can* simply say, "Hey friend . . . I miss your

face. Dinner Thursday?" You *can't* send passive aggressive "Fine" texts when they decline plans. If you get really hurt, have a frank discussion about it. If all goes well, you'll need to permanently accept the new balance between love and friendship in your friend's life. The sooner you become a part of the peaceful balance, the better.

If you break any of these ground rules, you owe your friend an apology. I know, it's tough to apologize; but if you want to stay close, you have to acknowledge the reality of how you each feel. Not apologizing is just another thing you'll have to apologize for.

You in a Relationship

Odds are, you also have a romantic life and aren't just cheering on your friend's. When you are in a relationship and your good friend is single, it's important that you also keep "Operation Accept and Support" in mind. This means . . .

Drop an Invite

It's important that you keep inviting your single friend to things, even if only couples will be there. The stereotypes about single people being bitter old witches who shrivel in the company of love is simply not true. When you're a kid, the cooties virus mainly pits girls against boys, but as you age, you'll find it keeps couples and singles from intermingling. Don't let cooties stand between you and friendship.

Let Her Vent

One thing you should never do is feel guilty or overwhelmed when your friend has a bad day because she's single. If she occasionally needs to vent to you about the anxiety that comes along with being single, don't assume that this is just permanently who she is now and that you'll never again have anything in common as long as you are in love. Common single anxieties your friend may have include: floating through life with no roots, general exhaustion with failed dates, and worrying about when she should text a date whose company she actually enjoyed. Everybody has good and bad days, no matter their relationship status; so plant your feet and hear your friend out like you would if she had any other issue. And then plan a movie date.

Be Careful Not to Lecture

Friendships naturally involve exchanging advice and tips, but when you are in a happy relationship, you need to be careful that your advice doesn't come off sounding smug or judgmental. Every relationship is different, so just because something worked for you, doesn't mean it'll work for somebody else. Instead, simply encourage your friend to follow her gut and think through her needs.

Honor Your Commitments

While you may have trouble dragging yourself away from a cuddle session, you'll never regret hanging out with your friend once you are in her presence. Plus, now you can spend some time venting about your relationship with someone who will laugh instead of getting defensive! Friends make your heart complete; they complete you.

Romantic relationships are never *actually* a threat to friendships. They may feel that way, depending on how much you and your friend had come to rely on each other in the framework of parallel single lives, but the people you date are just another aspect of your friendship. Dating is just one of the things you'll support each other through on the path to finding balance in your lives. If all goes well, you'll share the first dance with your friend on her wedding day! Just kidding—let your friend share the first dance with whomever it is she just married; then get in there and dance the second.

Frenemies: Stealth Friend Competitions

The "frenemy" is a movie archetype as quintessential to cinema as the bloodthirsty shark. *Death Becomes Her*; *Bride Wars*; *You, Me, and Dupree*—usually these movies star Goldie Hawn or her daughter, Kate Hudson. A frenemy is basically a person whom you are outwardly friendly with, but whose presence in your life causes you turmoil, either by making you doubt your worthiness or question your worldview. But before you just write off frenemies as evil villains, think back on what you may not have accomplished thus far in your life were it not for some healthy competition or challenging of your personal status quo. Perhaps watching your friend's enthusiasm for her career inspired you to go back to school. Maybe his laid-back attitude towards life and his definition of success has helped you put the headaches of your day-to-day job into perspective. While you may wish they'd fail just once so you can feel briefly superior, recognize those feelings as petty, and don't act on them. Feeling pangs of jealousy when your friends do well is normal. Try not to feel guilty about a feeling so automatic it is impossible to ignore; it's how you use those feelings that matters. Learning to maintain your friendships, even when you feel threatened, is important to your development. Friends who challenge you to think outside the box are important to finding happiness because they push you to understand what it takes to scale hurdles and, sometimes, help you learn from your failures gracefully—without disparaging those who succeed. So how do you approach this friendly competition with grace?

- If a close friend is doing well, let her inspire you, and hold your tongue when you feel petty. However, if an acquaintance is doing well, you can give in just a bit more to the jealousy you feel by confiding in your other close friends how hungry you are for the same achievements. Envy is the next best thing to a motivational speaker, should you need a healthy firing up.
- If your friend is doing well and you think she is rubbing that success in your face, take a step back and unravel your insecurities from the mix. Most likely your friend is just trying to brag about her achievements, not cut you down. If she is cutting you down, cut her out.
- Don't keep score. You'll know a healthy, perhaps unspoken, competition between friends has gone overboard when you find yourself holding grudges and feeling depressed. To cool down, talk out your feelings with an impartial friend.
- If you've permanently crossed the line from motivated to depressed, you may need to take a breather from the friendship; whether your friend is *trying* to make you feel this way or not, it doesn't matter. Look out for yourself—she'll understand. Kate Hudson is very understanding. (She *is* Kate Hudson, right?)

The more you use your friends for motivation and tap into the part of yourself that is proud of them, the more you'll realize how tiny, inconsequential, and silly those feelings of envy really are, beyond sparking your primal urge to compete.

One of the biggest threats to tipping the balance between friendly motivation and self-destructive jealousy is social media. Social media is like the Vaseline older television stars apply to their camera lens in order to look blurry and young again—even the most shriveled life can look glamorous. The trick is to limit social media's negative impact on your psyche and your friendships.

TWENTYSOMETHING FACT(ish)

Woody and Buzz Lightyear lit up the silver screen as lovable frenemies in *Toy Story*. Off screen, they were mortal enemies hell-bent on destroying each other.

Social Media

As you reach your late twenties, social media becomes a place where your frenemies are giving birth and your crazy uncle is passing around a petition for his state to secede from the United States. Social media is the number one thing twentysomethings love to complain about while also secretly loving it so much that they pretty much want to marry it. You hate that stalking now dominates your downtime, but love that Facebook allows you to share with the people in your life. It's like P90X; you hate it but you love it. It's like McDonald's—you know it's unhealthy but "Gimme those French fries."

When it comes to social media, there are just too many things in one place: past, present, and future. The social anxiety it brings can be crippling if you let it. A 2013 study by the University of Michigan found that the more young twentysomethings use Facebook, the worse they feel, and the harder it is for them to enjoy life in the moment. This means the more you share, the more your personal satisfaction will become entangled with the approval of your friends. This adds a new kind of pressure on your friendships—to always hit "like" lest you seem like you don't care, to see a "check-in" you were never invited to attend, to look happy with your life without seeming boastful, to see new friendships blossom from a distance and feel vaguely threatened. To put it simply—social media makes it feel like everyone is having fun without you.

QUARTERLIFE PRO TIP: SOCIAL MEDIA BLUES

Next time you see a picture of your friends on Instagram that you feel left out of, pull yourself out of the Internet world and into the real world by texting your friends to say you miss them. Don't live in the shadows; you are not the Phantom of the Opera.

These are all stresses you must try not to indulge . . . and not by becoming one of those people who refuses to join Twitter or Instagram. No, social media isn't going anywhere. It is a tool now for keeping in touch with family, receiving party invites, and probably other stuff, too. You can't keep thinking of it as a playground for stalking and pity partying. In your twenties, it's time to face Facebook like a grownup! So how do you do it? How do you make your trips to the Internet friendlier for everyone and keep social media from getting in your head, negatively impacting your friendships? See the following list for some advice:

- **Don't de-friend people.** It's Duh-rama! I get why it's tempting, but be chill. You agreed to be his friend in the first place. That's on you. Plus, it's very likely you have mutual friends you need to take into consideration. Are you going to walk up to that person in real life and tell him he isn't your friend now? Instead of being dramatic, just censor what he can see, and then block him from your timeline.
- **Stay out of it.** If you see a political fight between your friends—or any other kind of crazy—going down on the Internet, just sorta turn around and leave the room before they notice you. By that I mean, slowly shut down your computer, turn off the lights, and be very quiet until you are sure the fight has passed. Beware of sticking your foot in your mouth around a friend you forgot might be watching.
- **Don't publish interactions with your friend's ex online.** I'm not saying don't talk to your friend's ex. What I'm saying is, don't do it right in your friend's face(book) when you know your friend is at home On-Demanding *CSI: Las Vegas* episodes, the shards of her shattered life looming dangerously close to her heart. If you are on the other side of that last equation and your friend is checking in at some location with your ex online, save yourself the sulking. Just call her up and be like, "Hey . . . what the heck?" If she is like, "I'm *not* sorry about the heck," then block her from your newsfeed. She does not sound like a great friend to have.

- **Forgive your friends who are annoying on Facebook.** You know them in real life. Judging someone based on his or her Facebook personality is like judging a pumpkin by eating a pumpkin pie. If you like cinnamon, pumpkins are going to seem like they really have their shit together based on that pie. If you hate cinnamon, oh my goodness, you're gonna wish your pumpkin-pie friend would just stop adding cinnamon already. But here's the thing—a pumpkin pie just is not a good representation of a pumpkin. It's all for show.

Basically, if you wouldn't say it or do it to all of your Facebook friends' faces, then maybe, just maybe, you shouldn't do it online. I guess I should have just said that from the git-go! Could have saved us all some time. Overall, the best approach to social media is to take a step back and imagine a scenario as a face-to-face interaction. Don't jealously stare at a friend's profile because that's self-destructive, and you wouldn't jealously stare at his face for long periods of time if you were in person. That'd be creepy. Just keep yourself in check by taking a step back into the real world whenever possible.

THINGS TO REMEMBER

It's not just a convenient theme for the movie *It's a Wonderful Life*; friends really do make life worth living. That's why it's important to make sure you pick friends you truly click with and make those friends feel special. Then, when things get rough, weather that storm. Your twenties are the first decade of your life during which you are actively choosing friends, so look alive and remember:

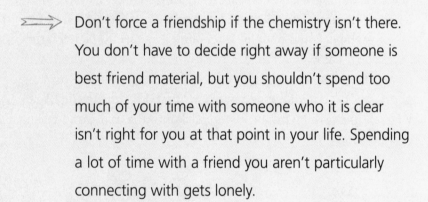

⟹ Don't force a friendship if the chemistry isn't there. You don't have to decide right away if someone is best friend material, but you shouldn't spend too much of your time with someone who it is clear isn't right for you at that point in your life. Spending a lot of time with a friend you aren't particularly connecting with gets lonely.

⟹ You have to ask new friends out on dates if you want to solidify your friendship. Hanging out in groups won't cut it in your twenties. Life is so crazy, people are looking for confidants instead of just drinking buddies. So start devoting one-on-one time to friends you love.

Friendships have hurdles. Even Bert and Ernie had their struggles—I'm sure Bert had some issues with the exorbitant amount of time Ernie seemed to spend in the bathtub. But you have to accept and keep your head on straight through the inevitable growing pains as you each balance new people in your lives and enjoy varying levels of success.

 Keep the pressures of social media at bay to assure they do not add unnecessary strain to your friendships. Social media is not real life; it is an intense, overly polished version of life. This means you shouldn't surrender your emotions to it the way you would in real life; if you feel anger or jealousy, take a step back.

CHAPTER 7

Debt—How You Got In and How You're Getting Out

ooming credit card debt, college loan debt, and good ol' fashioned negative bank account balances are some of the first things you become aware of when you realize life in your twenties is spinning out of control. It's the kind of debt you can't seem to make a dent in. Debt you used to ignore so easily. Remember the good old days? When you started an alarming amount of sentences with, "Well, when I'm rich . . . " or "I'll just put stuff on the credit card 'til payday . . . "? You probably thought you could test your limits and figure out the details later, but now there's a good chance that you're scrambling for any way at all to get out of debt.

Scrambling may feel productive, but getting out of debt is a slow, methodical process that you need to take on now so you don't have to deal with it as you move forward with your adult life. There are sneaky factors that likely continue to contribute to your debt, which you may be slow to see. Things like spur of the moment purchases and services you no longer need but forgot are being charged to your credit card on a monthly basis. But debt is just numbers, right? Why exactly is debt bad? Well, it leads to bad credit, which can:

- Prevent you from getting loans for everything from a house to schooling
- Increase interest rates on credit cards and loans
- Increase the cost of your cell phone plan, or prevent you from even getting one
- Lead to incessant calls from debt collectors
- Prevent a landlord from renting to you
- Plant fear in the heart of anyone wishing to marry you and legally incur your debt

It takes a full seven years from your original delinquency date for negative information to disappear from your credit rating. Seven years! Apparently, creditors hired the same judge who assigns bad luck to mirror breakers.

Throughout this chapter you'll find money saving tips, big and small, ranging from contributing to your 401(k) to skipping dessert at the restaurant. You'll also get info on identifying sneaky budget wasters, living a happy life frugally, and what, exactly, all those numbers on your paycheck mean. But the best way to kick off this budget revolution is to make one very important attitude adjustment—accept that you are not simply being thrifty; you are *broke*. Keep that in mind as we go over the fun part—how you probably got into this mess in the first place.

GETTING INTO DEBT IS FUN: BUT WHERE IS THE MONEY GOING?

Understanding where your money goes is the first step towards getting out of debt, so it's important for you to realize that there are two main phases of squandering money in your twenties. The first phase of debt starts as you begin to earn money out of college, and your student loans are still something you pretend doesn't exist. Because you aren't counting the money you owe on credit, you feel rich! And since you see money coming in, you feel that you've finally hit that glorious time in your life when you can buy nice, brand-new couches and cute shoes. In reality, as impatient as you may feel, you should use this time to bulk up your savings account while evaluating exactly how much money you have after purchasing the necessities. With every new job and raise will come an adjustment period where you must weigh the amount of money you are *actually* taking home versus the amount of extra money you *excitedly convince yourself* you have.

The next phase of debt often comes after the reality of your take-home pay (the amount you earn after taxes) sets in. You are working extremely hard and earning less than you feel you should. Since your paychecks aren't fulfilling you, you figure your credit cards will. Since you work hard, you think you deserve a $3 coffee every morning. Or, like me, you think you deserve luxurious 1,000 count sheets—so much so that you don't bother to check their price before heading to the register. You invest in *things* you want when you really need to invest that money in a savings account.

Both of these phases have one thing in common: willful ignorance.

If you can't celebrate your first job out of school with a fabulous life and silky bedding, you may be wondering, how *can* you pamper yourself? The answer to that is by relaxing with some chocolate milk and a romantic comedy from time to time—or maybe a $12 bottle of wine and *Breaking Bad*. Basically any combination of enjoyable beverage and cheap entertainment is about all you can afford. Don't feel like a failure—being broke is normal in your twenties. There was a time when you could put away money in a high interest savings account yielding 9 percent interest a year. These days, you are lucky to find one with .75 percent interest (note that decimal point), so saving real (nice couch) money takes a while. Welcome to your future.

REAL LIFE SURVIVAL STORY
Red Numbers

My good friend Jason moved to London for work shortly after college. As you can imagine, and have most likely experienced, a 22-year-old out in the world for the first time, cut off from the friends and family who know him best, does not exactly think long-term. Jason's only focus was kicking ass and taking names—of future contacts who could help his career flourish.

In the evenings, Jason kept pace with his new contacts at local pubs and looked the part by dressing up for the promotion he soon hoped to get. As hard as he worked at his career, he never quite found the time to understand how much money he was actually making. Maybe it was just the conversion rate of dollars to pounds, but to Jason, it seemed that no matter how much money he spent, his bank account kept growing. It was fantastic! This, he thought, must be what it feels like to be an adult. Until one fateful day, after nearly a year of working hard and playing harder, he realized his checking account balance wasn't red just for design reasons—red represented a negative number. It wasn't his savings that was growing; it was his debt. It took Jason eight years to bounce back and start saving. It took ten years for him to finally laugh that story off.

Aside from a misunderstanding about what it means to be "in the red," there are a few other factors that tend to lead twentysomethings into debt. Let's get the big one out of the way—flat-out misunderstanding your paycheck.

All Those Numbers on Your Paycheck

You may feel good about your salary or hourly wage, but brace yourself—Uncle Sam will be taking about a third of your paycheck in the form of taxes. It varies state to state, but these taxes can include: Federal, State, and City income tax, and Social Security and Medicare taxes. If you don't buy health insurance, you will have to pay a tax for that, as well. At the end of the year, you may be entitled to a small refund after filing your taxes, but, for the most part, this money is gone. Well, not gone—it's helping to make your country great and stuff, but you won't see it again in your bank account. If you *don't* see these taxes deducted from your paycheck, you have not outsmarted the system. This most likely means you are a "freelancer," and you'll have to pay these taxes at the end of the year; so prepare by putting at least one third of your freelance paycheck into savings. You could also choose to pay quarterly, which is less of a burden. Sounds like common sense, but I've never known a freelancer under the age of twenty-five who didn't get this math wrong at least once.

Another reason your paycheck might be smaller than you were expecting is your benefits. These benefits could include: dental, medical, vision, retirement, and any other benefit for which you willingly signed up. These are all taken out of your paycheck before taxes to save you from being taxed on those amounts each pay period. Finally! An area of your paycheck over which you have some control and can take advantage. While you could invest in these benefits outside of your paycheck, then just write them off at the end of the year, it's much easier—especially if you're living paycheck to paycheck—to deduct them immediately. If you aren't sure where to sign up for any of the following voluntary, pretax benefits, ask your HR person. If you are a freelancer, hold on to all of your receipts, and be sure to write off these common expenditures every time you do your taxes.

TWENTYSOMETHING FACT(ish)

The strong, persistent current of the Potomac River, which runs through Washington, D.C., is fed, in large part, by the tears of twentysomething freelancers who neglected to put away money for taxes.

Health Insurance (Including Dental and Vision)

As we discussed in Chapter 4, choose a plan that reflects your health needs. If you are a healthy twentysomething who sees doctors only for checkups and emergencies, pick a plan that reflects that so you aren't losing more of your money per pay period than necessary.

Medical Flex Spending Account

A medical Flex Spending Account (FSA) is an account in which you can set aside money, pretax, for medical purposes. You choose how much money to put in a medical FSA. Your insurer will give you that amount in the account upfront, and then it will be gradually taken out of your paycheck throughout the year, pretax. With most medical FSAs, you can immediately save 30 percent on everything related to your health: from contact solution to condoms to emergency room visits. There are only two catches: First, if you don't spend the money within the year, you don't get it back; so plan ahead. Second, some purchases may require a doctor's note. So if your doctor suggests you sit on a yoga ball to relieve back pain, be sure to ask for a note before you purchase that ball.

Commuter Flex Spending Account

A commuter FSA works just like a medical FSA, though it is perhaps more predictable. Getting to work is a professional expense and is, therefore, tax deductible. While you probably won't find any companies that will cover gas, they will get you that immediate, pretax discount (roughly 30 percent, depending) on parking and public transportation costs. Many will even cover the cost of buying and maintaining a bicycle!

401(k)

A 401(k) is an optional plan that takes a small percentage of your earnings and invests it in reliable stocks so you can get your money—with generous interest—back when you retire. It's important to start contributing to a 401(k) as soon as you can, early in your career. That way, you'll have money when you are a fabulous, elderly minx trying to find your third husband during bingo night at the retirement home. Most companies will match up to a certain percent of your contribution, so your goal should be to at least hit the maximum percentage they match—most likely between 3–5 percent of your paycheck.

Once you understand and have organized where your money goes before it even hits your bank account, the next step is to wrap your head around what happens to the money you can actually get your hands on. Most likely it is slipping right through your fingers because of sneaky budget wasters.

QUARTERLIFE PRO TIP: GENERIC AND IN-NETWORK

If you want to save hundreds of dollars a year, stay in-network when choosing your doctors. In-network means that you can see any doctor covered by your provider for only a small copay—you should ask if they take your insurance over the phone while making the appointment. Your provider may pay only a percentage of your visit to an out-of-network doctor—or not pay at all—depending on the plan. Staying in-network makes checkups and preventative care affordable and helps keep small health issues from spiraling into a larger expense. Also, choose generic prescription and over-the-counter drugs. Once the patents expire on everyone's favorite brand-name drugs, affordable generics hit the market with the same ingredients and health benefits. If you're nervous about ditching your favorite, well-advertised drug, just ask your doctor or even your local pharmacist to calm your fears.

Sneaky Budget Wasters

Even after ditching your willful ignorance and taking time to understand exactly how much money you are truly taking home in your paycheck, you may still find your debt accumulating. Or perhaps there's a few thousand dollars hanging out atop your credit card statement that you can't quite seem to knock out. This is the point where it helps to truly evaluate your spending and figure out where that money is going.

To start, think in terms of two- and four-week periods, like your pay periods, instead of calculating in months. Months are an odd-ball time period and harder to calculate. Sure, examining your money in four-week increments may cause you to overestimate how much you spend on regular monthly bills, because if months were an even four weeks long there would be thirteen of them in a year, but what's so bad about overestimating? Are you afraid you may find yourself pleasantly surprised by a few hundred extra dollars at the end of the year?

But I digress. Break down how much money you took in during those four weeks after taxes and benefits. Then, using your credit card and checking account statements, break down where your money has gone into five categories:

1. Bills (rent, Internet, electric, car payments)
2. Food and Home (groceries, take-out, cleaning supplies, toiletries)
3. Social (movies, bar tabs, restaurant meals, ATM withdrawals)
4. Splurges (clothes, computer, rug, manicures)
5. Savings

Within those categories, you should start to see where your overages are and set a reasonable budget for each of them based on your take-home pay, cutting your "Splurge" budget down to the bone. Conventional wisdom says you should try to put at least 10 percent of your take-home pay into savings, steadily increasing that percentage as your pay increases. But don't beat yourself up if you can't seem to save that much money while you're also trying to get out of debt. You're a twentysomething, not a doctor, damn it! So just do your best to save *something*. Once you get some savings socked away, you should celebrate with a nice, strong fist pump in the air.

After you've worked out your budget for the five categories, stick to it by monitoring your spending online and by writing reminders in your planner as we discussed in Chapter 2. Don't be too exact; try to overestimate what you are spending and underestimate how much you can afford. Then, try to learn as you spend so your budget will feel less like abstract numbers on paper and more like a lifestyle. Did those $3 coffees end up putting you $60 over budget for the last four weeks? Good to know—and fix—for the next four weeks. Be on the lookout for the following "Sneaky Budget Wasters," which could throw you off balance in the long run.

QUARTERLIFE PRO TIP: SOCIAL CURRENCY

When you go out and just want to have fun without worrying too much about spending, use cash so you can hold yourself easily accountable as you watch the money dwindle. This also allows your friends to make the classic, "Did you just come from a strip club?" joke when they see your wallet is full of singles. Everybody wins!

Sneaky Payments

Maybe you signed up for a free month of Hulu and forgot to cancel it before they started charging you. Perhaps you didn't read the fine print on the site you used to do a quick credit check and now they are regularly billing you. Maybe, as a joke, you bought "Charliesheeniswinning.com" back when that was a thing, and now it's only a thing on your bank statement. If you find a sneaky payment that automatically bills your account each month, call and cancel it immediately. It may take some time, but figuring out where and how to cancel bogus payments is worth it. Usually you can cancel by visiting the company website, but calling the company and speaking to a live representative is the best way to convince them to cancel a monthly payment you may have already been charged for. If you aren't sure where the charge is coming from, Google the name as it appears on your credit card or bank statement. You probably aren't the only one who's had mysterious-looking charges from that company show up on your bill—it's usually the company that snuck their fee into the fine print. Think of it this way—would you rather keep paying for a goofy web domain you don't use or, one fine day, have the freedom to buy your favorite kind of cereal, even if it's not on sale that week? Every twentysomething should pick cereal here. That's the dream.

Grabbing "Just One Beer" . . . and More

When you are a twentysomething and life is uncertain, leaving a night out with friends feels like leaving your childhood home all over again. You may go to bed and rest successfully—or you may just feel like a lonely failure for the rest of eternity. So, with that attitude in mind, you may decide to order more beers whether or not an evening is worth going into debt over. How can you make a change? Every night out, even on weekends, stop drinking around 10. When the clock strikes 10, drink some water. Assess the situation. Sobering up just a touch will help you stop being dramatic about how lonely the world is. Look around you. Do you want to go all in tonight or do you maybe want to save up for a bar tab and taxi home another night? Unless your skee ball arm is on fire this fine evening, consider heading home and transferring that money to savings.

Sneaky Fees

Sneaky fees are fees that you may have forgotten to account for. For example, forgetting to transfer money to checking before an auto payment comes out of your account can cost you up to $50 in overdraft fees from the bank. That is a lot of grocery money. Also, interest and late fees on the thousands of dollars you can't quite kick from your credit card bill can end up costing you hundreds of extra dollars by the end of the year. When it comes to your money, be sure to stay vigilant. As we discussed in Chapter 2, pull out your planner and write down the date of every auto payment so you can double check the money. Make sure you know when your credit card payments are due so you can dodge fees. Lastly, until you pay off your credit card debt, you *don't have* a disposable income—everything must go towards cleansing that debt. You shouldn't have a splurge category and your social category should give you just enough cash to keep you in good spirits. Try to put at least a couple hundred dollars in your rainy day fund, but, after you've eaten and paid bills, put the rest of your money towards your credit card.

QUARTERLIFE PRO TIP:
HOW TO CALCULATE CREDIT CARD INTEREST

To figure out how much interest you can expect to accrue while slowly chipping away at your credit card debt, just Google, "how to calculate credit card interest." There are a number of free calculators on the web. Once you've selected the dollar amount you can afford to pay off each month, these calculators will also let you know how long it will take you to completely pay off this debt. It's nice to know the exact location of the light at the end of the tunnel!

Breaking Up with a Live-In Lovah

We're not talking about the emotional cost here. Live-in breakups are financial nightmares and never something you've planned for. Hopefully you have a rainy day fund so you can put money towards moving, buying new furniture, and re-buying all the odds and ends you forgot you needed—right down to the maple syrup and toilet brush. Yet, even if you don't have a rainy day fund, you can't delay this storm. Leaving a living situation that is costing you emotionally is worth the financial discomfort (and it gives you a good reason to keep your heart in check next time).

Instead of staying in a bad situation, go into preplanned debt. This is not debt at the hands of willful ignorance—this is debt you are going into with a plan to control. First of all, as much emotional pain as you may be in, make sure to divide up joint purchases fairly with your ex. Be strong. Next, you will not be purchasing anything you don't absolutely need for a while—even that $12 bottle of wine. This is a time in your life when, as independent and stubborn as you are, you absolutely need to ask for help (and wine). Letting your friends know what you are going through will allow them to keep their ears open for a good deal on an apartment, second-hand furniture, and a place for you to crash while you figure things out. When it's time to start purchasing odds and ends, plan your budget carefully—otherwise, Bed Bath & Beyond can add up fast. About a month after you've established your new living situation, restructure your budget to pay off your credit card as soon as possible.

Cable or, God Forbid, Premium Cable!

Television may feel like your best friend; it's always there for you and provides background noise while you are tidying up or trying to teach yourself how to braid your hair. In that light, cable may feel like a necessity and not a "Sneaky Budget Waster." But trust me, if you are in debt, this friend is doing you more harm than good.

This may feel like your Everest, but it's time to cancel your cable. You must persevere and find the ol' lemonade in the cloud. (That's the saying, right? Good.) You may discover that you never truly knew your flesh-and-bone friends until you've invited yourself over for their cable and stayed for the squeal-filled terror you both suffer at the hands of a random *Celebrity Ghost Stories* marathon.

An Unused Gym Membership

Many people tell themselves, even if they aren't going regularly, that they haven't truly failed on their personal health goals until they officially cancel their gym membership. Seeing that monthly charge on your credit card bill feels like a necessity—a promise to your health and well-being. But it's also a lot of money, so . . . if you haven't been to the gym for an entire month, even though you've been in town, cancel that membership. Did you ever consider that gyms aren't for you? Don't join a gym if you don't already like gyms. If you're just going to go there and half ass it, if you go at all, why bother? Instead, learn how to work out on your own. Try a few sessions with a personal trainer to make sure you know what you're doing; then try videos, podcasts, running, etc. You're much more likely to sweat and work out so hard that your face looks stupid if you're not in public, anyway.

Small Impulse Buys

Have you ever spent forty-five minutes at Target picking out the perfect shade of eye shadow, unwilling to spring for more than one out of respect for your ailing budget, only to find yourself unable to pass by a refrigerator full of ice-cold Cokes on your way to the register? Have you ever said, "That Madewell sale is too good to ignore; might as well buy one more boxy top"? Or what about Kickstarter? Did you black out with excitement at the idea of your favorite cancelled television show turning into a movie; then wake up to find your credit card debt $40 deeper?

Resist the urge to step outside your budget, especially in the splurge category. There is actually a very simple way to know whether you are *irresponsibly* splurging or spending on something that is actually a necessity. Before you make the purchase, say out loud, "I have to buy this." If you frown as you say this, you are probably making a good decision. If you smile or if your eyes feel crazy and wild, put away your wallet.

There are a lot of factors that can lead you into debt—whether it's willful ignorance, general confusion about your paycheck, or a blind spot in the way of sneaky budget wasters. Whatever it may be, your eyes should be open now, and your budget should be set. So let's dig deeper and take a look at how you can indulge in the things that make you happy while remaining on a twentysomething budget.

LIVING HAPPILY ON A TWENTYSOMETHING BUDGET

Once you've cut out all of the indulgences you can't afford, your future for the next few years—or however long you need to pay off your debt and beef up your savings account—may seem bleak. You're young, and you want to enjoy it while you can. That's understandable. But, assuming you also want to enjoy the rest of your life and set yourself up for success in your thirties and beyond, you have to stick to economically responsible fun. Nerd alert. I know. Let's take a look at what are probably some of your favorite activities and figure out how you can enjoy them on a budget.

Vacationing on the Cheap

Vacations are important for your mental health and your soul. Once your budget is under control, even if you are still on a strict payment plan to get fully out of debt, planning a trip is a fair investment. But beware—even after you've got a good deal on a flight and hotel, vacations are full of small costs that add up, so you'll need to plan carefully.

The first thing you'll need to do is begin to regularly put a portion of your paycheck in your vacation fund and leave it there—no cheating. While this may require cutting back even further during indulgent nights out at the bars, the excitement of getting out of town should be enough to keep your spirits high. If you are a social person, invite a big group on your vacation; splitting the cost will make it cheaper, and you'll hit a nice, social high.

When planning your travel, look for bus trips that have gotten good reviews or book your airline ticket at least three months in advance. Booking a week in advance can also be cheap, but not as reliable. When flying, pack light so you can carry your luggage on—airlines these days charge for every bag you check and charge more if the bag is heavy. You can't take water through security, unfortunately, but you can bring small, packaged snacks, which will help you save money if you get hungry while you wait at your gate—assuming you don't mind your food being x-rayed. If you rent a car, try to invite enough friends to comfortably fill that car to cut down the cost. Also, check your credit card agreement; you may already be covered and will not need to buy the daily rental insurance offered by the car rental company.

The most affordable vacations involve nature, so avoid big cities and their inflated bottled-water and transportation prices. Drag your friends to a lake house or beach. There, you can split the cost of groceries and eat your meals without having to figure out the tip. If you do eat out, get the early bird special with all the old people. They are wise. You aren't stuck at work, so take advantage of the cheap eats. You may even find your day-to-day expenses are actually cheaper when you leave home!

If you must go to the city, go for it with the cheesy bus tours and goofy tourist T-shirts; this is easy, preplanned fun, which takes the pressure off of you to find your way. But when it comes to your meals, do some research and eat off the grid. Those city folk around the tourist areas know you've been on your feet all day, know you are hungry, and can't wait to charge you more than twice what everything is worth. Carry a small bag so you can keep your belongings nearby and won't have to purchase small things as you go. And, most importantly, relax. That's the point.

Eating on the Cheap

The easiest way to eat on a budget is to buy all of your food at the grocery store. But it's not just about walking through the doors of the supermarket instead of a restaurant; it's about embracing the fact that if blueberries are on sale this week, you are going to be eating a lot of blueberries even if you were hoping to get strawberries. There are street smarts, there are the water-cooler smarts we learned about in Chapter 3—and then there are grocery-aisle smarts. It takes a while to figure out how to optimize your grocery store savings, but it's worth the effort. Here are a few tips.

- When stocking up on fresh fruit, remember that apples and oranges stay fresh twice as long as berries and bananas, so enjoy the food with a shorter shelf life first.
- Other than some vitamin C and B_1, frozen fruits and vegetables do not lose much nutritional value when compared to the "fresh" ones that go through shipping—so if you need more time with your produce, supplementing with frozen is a smart, thrifty option.
- Remember to double check sell-by dates in the dairy aisle. Sometimes you'll find milk that is a week or two "younger" than the one next to it. Don't buy that cougar milk—pick up that young gold-digger instead.
- Unless cooking is a hobby of yours you take extremely seriously, don't try out recipes that require ingredients you won't be using again like, say, dill. I think about this lesson every time I finally use my fancy red wine vinegar—to kill fruit flies.

For a while, you may find yourself buying too much; maybe you'll even have to watch a few bananas wither in your fruit bowl before you have a chance to eat them. It's a painful process, but stick with it, and you will save your health and your budget.

QUARTERLIFE PRO TIP: MISFIT FOOD WEEK

If you want to be a super-saver, every few weeks, don't go to the grocery store. Celebrate misfit food week. Just finish the pasta, cans of soup, and week-old broccoli that's been winkin' at you from the crisper. Up for a real challenge? Interpret "sell-by" dates as a comfortable distance from "eat-by" dates, which you assign however you see fit. Trust your nose; finally empty those cabinets and save! That said, when in doubt, throw it out. If there is a new kind of odor you can't quite place, your hard-saved money will go to the same place you will—the emergency room.

Dating on the Cheap

So you want some romance, do you? Here's the thing about romance—it can be pretty expensive. Think about it—candle-lit dinners, bear skin rugs, movie popcorn. These things can wreck your bank account, but there are ways to find romance on a twentysomething budget. Unless you are going on dates with an Internet wunderkind who made millions inventing a technology we don't yet understand (Skynet, yikes!), odds are your date will be thankful you are thrifty. After a few dates, you'll most likely be splitting the bill.

Pick a restaurant with affordable entrées and dim lighting that can pass for candlelight. Don't skimp on mood lighting. If it costs you two dollars more per entrée, budgets be damned! There's at least one semi-romantic and affordable location in every town. Know where you are going beforehand so you can research. This way, you won't meet up together and end up nervously settling on a place you can't afford. If you feel pushy always suggesting one optimal place based on your research, try suggesting a few options you think could work so your date doesn't go off the rails and pick somewhere pricey. Don't be shy about discussing your budget; conventional wisdom says not to begin a relationship with lies. Be coy. Say, "That's a little rich for my blood." Then wink. (Wink!) Just from personal experience, whatever you do, do not go to a tapas restaurant. Tapas means "still hungry and now also broke" in English.

If you are at the restaurant enjoying your time so much that you don't want it to end, but you become worried you'll spend too much on drinks, suggest getting the check and continuing your conversation at a dive bar nearby. This is where your research comes in handy—find nearby drink specials in advance. Ask for the check immediately after your entrées are finished. Don't get dessert at the restaurant. There is always some kind of holiday candy at Duane Reade or CVS that has just gone on sale. What are you? Too good for Peeps? What kind of diva is your sweet tooth, Queen Elizabeth?

Day dates are also a great option for the budget-minded twentysomething. Picnics can last as long as you like, and, thanks to your tax dollars, parks are free and plentiful. As with vacations, nature is a twentysomething's best friend. Look for fun events you can take long romantic walks through, like flea markets, museum exhibits, or, I dunno, polka festivals. After all, it doesn't actually matter what's going on around you, as long as there is something distracting enough to fill any awkward silences.

REAL LIFE SURVIVAL STORY
Being Honest about Being in Debt

In my mid-twenties, the economy crashed, my overtime was cut, and I faced a sudden, dramatic pay cut. I wasn't quick enough to cut back my already indulgent spending (1,000 count sheets, people), so my debt skyrocketed. Acknowledging that money was anything but numbers would have sent me into a full-on meltdown, so I went into denial. I never thought of myself as "broke." I suppose I had the comfort of knowing that if things really went downhill, I could just hop on the next bus back to Cleveland, assume a tearful, fetal position against my mom's bosom, and move back in to my childhood bedroom. So instead of truly cutting back, I chose to be "thrifty" and do extremely minor things to save money—like refuse to get drinks with people I already didn't like.

Around this time, I found myself dating the most upbeat man I'd met in my life. He wasn't chipper in an obnoxious way, just calm and steady with a smile so easy to get I felt like I was a standup comedian. A few dates in, the money conversation finally came up. He *brought* it up. He confessed that he really wanted to see me but could not afford to take me to the movies. In all my years surrounded by broke twentysomethings, I'd never heard anybody admit that so plainly. I decided to make him feel better by telling him how much I admired his thriftiness. He cut me off, "I'm not thrifty, Mary, I'm broke." He had a smile across his face that told me everything was going to be okay. The pressure I'd felt throughout my twenties to impress—to order rounds of shots for my friends and impulse-buy cool jackets—suddenly felt silly. I had been spending money that wasn't mine—money that, if anything, belonged to my future self. Seeing my situation through the eyes of the happiest person I'd ever met—who had no issues admitting he was a broke, work in progress—allowed me to relax and clearly look at my horrifying credit card statement for the first time. It was . . . well, horrifying.

The truth is, you aren't just trying to save money in your twenties—you are broke. You don't have much of a disposable income at all, as much as you'd like to believe otherwise. If you think you've carved out a couple hundred dollars of wiggle room in your budget, you'll probably find out next month that you simply did the math wrong. It's okay. You're not alone. When it comes to a quarterlife crisis, you are sadly never, ever alone.

Dressing on the Cheap

As you progress through your twenties, it will most likely become more important to you to look put-together in your day-to-day life. Whether this is due to the pressures of a corporate job or the desire to look like a catch on dates, sneakers and hoodies—as affordable as they are—just don't cut it anymore. The trick is to find fashion on a budget.

There are a lot of tips out there about how to execute fashion on a budget, many of them presented by retailers trying to sell off their leftover winter items to make room for summer. But the most experienced fashionistas will tell you the only "trick" is to spend a fair amount on a select few wardrobe pieces you know you'll love and avoid the temptation to splurge on sale items you might just never want to wear again. Don't go for high-end, runway items; just don't worry so much about whether or not the one piece you love is on sale. Then, once you've bought those few, lovable pieces you've had your eye on, try not to shop at all until they fall apart.

So how do you know which splurges you'll love? Take some time to know your personal style. Do you like earth tones or are you fearless in the face of bold colors? Do you prefer boxy tops or do you prefer a more fitted look? In a nutshell, what do you feel the most comfortable and confident wearing? Don't go out on fashion limbs when you are trying to save money. If you are in the dressing room thinking, "I'm a little uncomfortable, but maybe it's time for a new look!" Then, no! That is not your new look. You'll probably never wear this. Your new look is a savings account. Also, while I'm on it, clean your closet before buying new clothes! Throwing out clothes you haven't worn in the past year helps you to get a sense of what looks are working for you, while also making room in your closet for the pieces you love.

TWENTYSOMETHING FACT(ish)

Forty-seven percent of twentysomethings have bought high-water pants with a zipper that doesn't stay up simply because they were on sale. Worth it?

Wardrobe Staples

There are a few staple items every wardrobe needs, and knowing what they are allows you to buy them when they are off-season or on sale and, at the very least, stepping outside these staple items will signal you've hit a stopping point to your shopping. If you are settling for a version of one of these staple items that you don't totally love just to save yourself twenty bucks, keep in mind that you might just end up shopping again when you realize you are fed up with wearing something you don't really even like. Don't waste money on things you don't like when it comes to the tent poles of your wardrobe. Find the basic pieces you love in a look that is classic and timeless; then mix and match freely with a few cheaper items that can be trendy since they probably won't last as long. This is what a lean, mean, professional, twentysomething wardrobe should look like:

- Versatile spring/fall jacket
- Super-warm winter jacket
- Couple of button-up shirts that fit well; one of them crisp and white
- Go-to dress for nice occasions with comfortable go-to heels
- Skirt in whatever style looks best on you (avoid patterns; we're talking basics)
- Three sweaters: casually loose, pro-tight, and one somewhere in between
- Couple of summer dresses you love
- Three pairs of pants in the style you prefer (cut jeans into shorts when they die)
- One plain, black cardigan
- Shoes: pair of boots, pair of ballet flats, and one pair somewhere in between

If you are in debt, do not allow yourself to shop unless you are straight up replacing one of these items—meaning you must throw one item out for every item you bring home. The best way to keep your chosen few items of clothing nice is to wash them about half as much as you think you should (socks and underwear excluded). Most of the wear and tear on the clothes you love happens in the wash. Washing by hand is ideal so you can make sure your clothes aren't getting dropped into those evil machines and beat up during the spin cycle.

The bottom line is that it is possible to live happily and look chic on a twentysomething budget. You can vacation, date, and eat well. Maybe your life won't look like it was ripped from a glamorous magazine, but at least you'll have a well-rested glow that can only come once you've released yourself from the stressful burden that is debt. It may take a while, but, as with any other rut, the first step is admitting you have a problem.

THINGS TO REMEMBER

When it comes to saving money, the lesson of this chapter is—be the mysterious tightwad. If you are at a large group dinner, throw in money, but don't factor in tax, tip, or the birthday boy/girl's portion. When people start to notice the bill is short, act surprised and look around at everyone else. Just kidding! *Don't do this*! This would make you the worst. This chapter is about thinking long-term to build your savings while maintaining your friendships and getting out of the debt that reckless spending may have gotten you into in the first place. As you work your way out of that debt, remember:

1. There aren't really quick fixes to getting out of debt; it is a steady, methodical process that you must commit yourself to if it's going to work. You have to ignore short-term satisfaction if you want to enter your thirties feeling like a baller.

2. Be on the lookout for sneaky budget wasters. Triple check your credit card statement to make sure you don't have recurring charges you forgot about or monthly fees you've been failing to calculate. Cancel

cable and your gym membership. Basically, look at your life, and make sure your bank statement is reflecting it accurately.

3. The truth is, you can live your life to the fullest, even on a twentysomething budget. Be mindful as you engage in things like vacation and dating to make sure the little things aren't adding up to a big bill. Take advantage of the great outdoors whenever possible—your tax dollars are already paying for them, after all!

4. Don't run from your problems or pretend you are something you are not—admit that you are broke and act accordingly. Honestly? Honesty is kind of hot.

AFTERWORD

Just Relax about Turning 30, Ya Nerd

Everybody is afraid of turning 30. It feels like the end of a quiz show. It feels like that moment when you have to put down your pen and commit to whatever you were able to write down before the *Final Jeopardy!* music ended—the final clue being "You learned this in your twenties." It's hard not to imagine Alex Trebek laughing as he reads your final answer aloud for the audience, "What is 'don't forget you used your bathrobe to mop up a soda spill last night'?"

But whatever you were able to jot down before the music ended, just relax about turning 30, ya nerd.

The most important reason to get it together during your quarterlife crisis is so that you can roll into thirty, free of this bullshit, with your head held high. You won't have it all figured out but at least you'll have kicked cumbersome habits and will own a mattress with clean sheets on it. Who cares if you don't "have it all" by thirty? All you need to do by thirty is set the stage—know in your gut what your most fulfilling career would be even if you're not quite there yet, have a workout routine in place and eat well, stop spending so much time with selfish lovers and awkward friends, stop frivolously spending, and know how to relax like a baller without spending like a fool.

A lot of twentysomethings like to assign age requirements to their goals, and a lot of times they decide that if they haven't hit a goal by thirty, they should give it up. Don't. If you've accomplished all of your dreams by thirty, what the hell are you going to do for the next 150 years of your life? Coast? Sounds boring. (I say 150 years because I'm assuming science will have replaced all of our organs with plastic in the next few decades.) If you set the stage in your twenties, moving forward, you'll be free to focus on yourself and the people you love. All the things you've struggled with in your twenties? Your goal is to make them old hat by thirty—things you can do in your sleep. Once you hit the new decade, you can change up your career; learn new skills; spend weekends filling your heart with memories, instead of your blood with alcohol; and you'll most likely be healthier than you've ever been. Your life isn't going to instantly become mundane with the big 3-0, and, if it does, it'll be because you want it that way.

INDEX

ABOUT THE AUTHOR

Mary Traina is a career-minded, single girl living in New York City. She writes a regular series for Zooey Deschanel's site, HelloGiggles, entitled *Late 20s Rut-Busting*. In it, she muses over the strength it takes to fix all of the bad decisions we tend to make in our twenties. Her writing has also been featured on *Refinery29* and *Huffington Post Women*. A graduate of Kent State University, Mary moved to New York City from Cleveland, Ohio, to pursue a career in television, starting with an internship at the *Late Show with David Letterman*. Mary now writes, produces, and edits television promos, most ridiculously for *Mega Shark vs. Crocosaurus* starring Jaleel White.